This book is dedicated to the memory of Rabbi Howard R. Greenstein. Rabbi Greenstein was a coauthor of this book but died prior to the book's publication. He was a much-beloved rabbi, a fine scholar and teacher, and highly esteemed by his colleagues and friends. He was dearly loved by his family. We are grateful for his life and his contributions, particularly to this book to promote religious understanding and God's *shalom* in this world.

# What Do Our Neighbors Believe?

## Questions and Answers on Judaism, Christianity, and Islam

Howard R. Greenstein

Kendra G. Hotz

John Kaltner

Westminster John Knox Press
LOUISVILLE • LONDON

*Book design by Sharon Adams*
*Cover design by Lisa Buckley*
*Cover photographs © Royalty-Free/Corbis and Jupiterimages*

*First edition*
Published by Westminster John Knox Press
Louisville, Kentucky

This book is printed on acid-free paper that meets the American National Standards Institute Z39.48 standard.♾

PRINTED IN THE UNITED STATES OF AMERICA

07 08 09 10 11 12 13 14 15 16—10 9 8 7 6 5 4 3 2

**Library of Congress Cataloging-in-Publication Data**

Greenstein, Howard R.
    What do our neighbors believe? : questions and answers on Judaism, Christianity, and
  Islam / Howard R. Greenstein, Kendra G. Hotz, John Kaltner.—1st ed.
      p. cm.
    Includes bibliographical references.
    ISBN-13: 978-0-664-23065-4 (alk. paper)
    ISBN-10: 0-664-23065-2 (alk. paper)
  1. Religions.   2. Judaism.   3. Christianity.   4. Islam.   I. Hotz, Kendra G.   II. Kaltner,
John.   III. Title.
    BL80.3.G74 2007
    200—dc22                                                              2006048984

# Contents

# Publisher's Note

*T*he neighbors we encounter these days do not always hold the same religious beliefs as we do. This is a fact of contemporary life, exemplified by the diversities of places of worship we see as we travel: synagogues, churches, and mosques.

Those with religious sensitivity realize that in today's culture it is important, on many levels, to understand what our neighbors believe. The book that follows seeks to provide easy access to beliefs of three major world religions: Judaism, Christianity, and Islam.

The nine chapters focus on the big, "umbrella" issues that are dealt with by these three faiths. Each chapter is composed of three questions with responses by experts on each of the three religions. The writers all have deep knowledge of the faith traditions and here write clearly and simply to acquaint us with the different viewpoints.

This book is designed for personal use as well as group study. Groups can examine a particular faith by reading the responses from that perspective in all the chapters. Or one can study the book by chapters, comparing and contrasting the three traditions on each issue. Helpful materials at the end of the book provide resources for further reflections.

We hope this book will open windows of understanding for those interested in three of the world's major faiths. Our knowledge of what our neighbors believe can enhance our own beliefs. It can also open us to new insights that can deepen our perceptions and tolerance in a world where "peace among the religions is the prerequisite for peace among the nations."[1]

Donald K. McKim for
Westminster John Knox Press

1. Hans Küng, *Theology for the Third Millennium: An Ecumenical View*, trans. Peter Heinegg (New York: Doubleday, 1988), 209.

Chapter One

# Origin and Composition

## 1. When, where, and how did the religion begin?

*Judaism.*  The story of Judaism, as does all history, begins with a dim and misty past. Little agreement exists among most historians about the actual beginning of Jewish civilization, including the period of the founding patriarchs, Abraham, Isaac, Jacob, and Joseph, or even the life of Moses, including the enslavement and liberation from bondage in Egypt. Traditionalists subscribe to every detail of the biblical narrative as historical fact. Others accept only the broadest contours of those events described in this earliest period of Israelite folklore, without ascribing to them any factual foundation.

The most reliable conjecture is that the gradual settlement of the Hebrews in Canaan (later called Palestine by the Romans, on behalf of the native Philistines) began sometime between 1300 and 1200 BCE. After a tenuous and contentious truce under the rule of the Judges for about two hundred years, the twelve separate tribes finally united and formed the first commonwealth, established first under Saul and then under David and Solomon about ten centuries before the Christian era.

After Solomon's death, as a result of internal conflict and division, Palestine was divided into two separate kingdoms. The larger was Israel, which included ten of the original twelve tribes, and the smaller was Judah, which consisted of the remaining two. In 722 BCE, the Assyrian Empire attacked and destroyed the northern kingdom of Israel, which marked the close of a pivotal era. Inasmuch as only Judah retained its independence, the defeat marked the end of Hebrew history and the beginning of Jewish history. The word *Jew* is simply a contraction of the word *Judean*.

Contrary to popular belief, the ten tribes of Israel were not "lost." They were obliterated as a nation. A number of well-meaning people remain convinced that somewhere a sizeable remnant continue to exist undetected. A few

1

even speculate that they may be linked to the Native Americans of North America. Such connections, however, have never been documented. The same applies to claims of their existence in Africa, South America, or the British Isles. For nearly another 150 years, Judah continued to survive as a small nation, leading a very precarious existence at the crossroads of powerful empires. Finally, in 586 BCE it too was laid waste by the overwhelming might of the Babylonian Empire. The capital, Jerusalem, was destroyed along with the Temple of Solomon, and most of its leadership sent into exile to Babylonia.

Ironically, these decisive centuries, though racked with bloodshed and chaos, produced the greatest visionaries of ancient Israel, the literary prophets. Such spiritual giants as Isaiah, Jeremiah, Amos, Micah, and Hosea not only gave Judaism its distinctive religious character but shaped the moral legacy of all Western civilization as well.

In 516 BCE, when numbers of exiles began returning from Babylon, the community established a Second Jewish Commonwealth and rebuilt Jerusalem, which continued for another six hundred tumultuous years. It struggled first under Persian rule, then under the Greeks and Syrians, and finally under Roman domination. It thrived briefly for nearly a century of independence under its own Hasmonean dynasty after the successful revolt of the Maccabees against the Greek-Syrian Empire in 168 BCE, which inspired the festival of Chanukah.

The revolt against the Roman Empire in 70 CE, however, ended in catastrophe. The Romans razed the Temple and demolished the city of Jerusalem. The Jews who were not slaughtered were expelled and dispersed throughout the known world. A few settled as far east as Central Asia, others settled in the hills of Ethiopia, and still others, in Italy and Spain. Although Egypt became for a time an important center of Jewish life, it was in Babylonia, that part of the world in which Abraham the first Hebrew patriarch was born, that a stable and thriving community grew and lasted for well over a thousand years. It was during that period and in that place that the Jewish people created and developed their major historic institutions, including the synagogue, the academies of higher learning, the Talmud, and the foundations of Jewish law.

Jews arrived in Europe as early as the time of Julius Caesar, although the community consisted of only scattered settlements until the eleventh century. The principal center of Jewish life at this juncture, however, was Islamic Spain. Jewish scholars, writers, and scientists under the benign rule of Muslims produced more philosophy, poetry, science, and religious literature during this era called the Golden Age than in any other period or place of its history.

A major turning point was 1492, with the expulsion of Jews from Christian Spain after a century of relentless and devastating persecution by the combined tyranny of both church and kingdom. They fled primarily to non-Catholic countries, including Holland and Turkey, but eventually the largest number settled in Eastern Europe, where a flourishing community emerged in spite of Czarist oppression. Jews there were essentially autonomous and self-contained, which permitted them to create incomparable institutions of learning, a stable family life, and at least a fair measure of economic security.

*Christianity.*    Christianity began early in the first century of the common era when Jesus of Nazareth began his ministry of preaching and healing in the Roman-ruled region of Palestine known as Galilee. Jesus was raised in a Jewish family, and when he began his public ministry at about the age of thirty, he did so in the custom of a rabbi, or teacher of Torah. He gathered disciples and taught them and the crowds who gathered around them wherever they traveled. He healed the diseased, called sinners to repentance, and offered forgiveness for sins. While upholding the importance of the law of Moses as an expression of the will of God, he also challenged conventional ways of interpreting it, especially when that interpretation marginalized social outcasts and those without power. While never directly challenging the authority of the Roman Empire, he called people to remember that their ultimate loyalty rested with the kingdom of God. He healed those who were diseased and raised others from the dead. He ate and conversed with the intellectuals and social elites of his day, but also with those deemed unworthy of his attention, such as women, tax collectors, and sinners. The Gospel according to Mark, one of the oldest written accounts of the birth of Christianity, says simply that "Jesus came to Galilee, proclaiming the good news of God, and saying, 'The time is fulfilled, and the kingdom of God has come near; repent, and believe in the good news'" (Mark 1:14–15).

Toward the end of his short public life, Jesus and his disciples traveled to Jerusalem to celebrate the Passover. While there Jesus challenged the religious authorities and came to the attention of the civil authorities, probably because of his teachings about a "kingdom" other than that of the Roman Empire. This attention from the Romans eventually led to his execution by crucifixion. Though Christians have long blamed the Jewish leaders for the death of Jesus, in fact, he was executed for a political crime, sedition. The charge against him, posted on a placard over his head on the cross, read, "King of the Jews." The early Christian community, eager to deflect negative attention from the Romans, muted the political nature of Jesus' crime and thereby contributed to what has become a long, horrible history of blaming the Jews for the death of Jesus and of persecuting them because of it. On the third day after his death, Jesus rose from the dead and appeared to his followers: first to the women, then to the twelve disciples, and finally to the crowds. After a time, he ascended bodily into the heavens.

The life, death, resurrection, and ascension of Jesus form the founding narrative of the Christian faith. The earliest followers of Jesus proclaimed his message of good news and proclaimed Jesus himself as the content of that good news when they affirmed that he was more than a wandering rabbi and healer. For Christians, Jesus of Nazareth is the Christ or Messiah, which means "the anointed one." Jesus came to be understood as the Son of God, as God Incarnate, as God-in-our-midst. The Nicene Creed, an early Christian affirmation of faith, declares that Jesus is "very God of very God." His mighty works point to the presence of the kingdom of God and to Jesus as the one who initiates it. The "good news" that the Gospels present is that through Christ, humanity can be reconciled to God. The early Christians gathered in private homes on the first day of the week, Sunday, the day of the resurrection, to share a meal commemorating the life, death, and resurrection of Christ, to read and proclaim Scripture, and to prepare themselves for Christ's return. They baptized new members into their fellowship, spread word of the gospel, and made provisions to care for the widows in their midst.

After the Romans crushed a Jewish rebellion in the year 70 and destroyed the Temple in Jerusalem, Christianity along with Judaism lost its status as a tolerated religion within the Roman Empire. Christians became subject to sporadic persecution that made it necessary to meet in secret and dangerous to proclaim their faith publicly. In the early fourth century, however, the emperor Constantine had a vision of the cross and heard a voice saying "in this sign conquer." Under the banner of the cross he won a decisive battle to become the sole Roman emperor and soon after issued an edict of religious tolerance that ended persecution of the Christian church. He later made Christianity the favored religion of the empire. The faith that began as a small, persecuted sect became the religion of the powerful. One result of this dramatic change in status has been that Christians have always struggled to understand and articulate how their faith ought to be related to culture.

*Islam.*    Islam traces its roots to the time of the Prophet Muhammad (570–632 CE), who is one of the most important and influential religious figures in human history. Muhammad lived his entire life in an area known as the Hijaz, which is found in the western portion of the Arabian Peninsula in what is now Saudi Arabia.

Very little is known about Muhammad's life prior to his prophetic career. He was orphaned at a young age and was raised by a paternal uncle named Abu Talib. He spent most of his life in Mecca, an economic and religious center that was the largest city in the Hijaz. Mecca was located on the main travel route that merchants took as they transported their goods to and from places as far away as India, and this meant many travelers and visitors would stop in the city to rest and replenish their supplies.

Mecca also attracted many guests because it housed the Kaaba, a religious shrine that was a popular pilgrimage destination. The dominant Arabian religion at that time was polytheism, and sources tell us that as many as 360 gods were housed in the Kaaba during the period just prior to the rise of Islam. Many Arabs would travel great distances to visit this holy site, particularly during those times of the year that were set aside for pilgrimage. Like the commercial travelers who passed through the city, this large influx of visitors required lodging, food, and other services, and they therefore had a very positive effect on the Meccan economy.

Like many Meccans, Muhammad made his living in commerce and trade. At the age of twenty-five he married his boss—she may have owned the company he worked for—a woman named Khadijah who was about fifteen years older than Muhammad. He never married another woman while she was alive, and she was a source of comfort and strength in the early years of his prophetic career.

The turning point of Muhammad's life occurred when he was about forty years old. According to Islamic sources, Muhammad frequently went off on his own to pray in a cave on Mount Hira. One day in the year 610, while he was engaged in prayer, a voice spoke to him and commanded, "Recite!" This was the first experience of what Muhammad and his followers would come to see as a series of revelations from God that would continue throughout the remaining twenty-two years of his life. The voice was understood to be that of the angel Gabriel, and the revelations would eventually be gathered together into a book that was called the Qur'an. After a period of initial confusion and doubt, Muhammad came to view himself as a prophet who had been chosen by God to deliver a message of monotheism to the people of Mecca, who were urged to leave behind their polytheistic ways and embrace worship of the one true God. The name given to this form of religion was *islam*, an Arabic term meaning "submission" that underscored the believer's attitude of surrender in the face of God's authority and power.

Muhammad's message was not well received in Mecca. He was able to gain a relatively small following, but many rejected it outright. There was a very pragmatic reason why some refused to accept his teaching: if they dismantled the polytheistic system currently in place, people would stop making pilgrimages to the Kaaba, and Mecca would lose a significant amount of income. Reactions became so hostile that Muhammad began to fear for the safety of his followers. The early Islamic sources contain many references to the threats and dangers Muhammad and the early Muslims endured at the hands of the Meccans.

Muhammad's fortune turned in 622, when the inhabitants of Yathrib asked him to come and live among them. Located about 250 miles north of Mecca, Yathrib had a significant Jewish population, and Muhammad had been invited to serve as a judge for the various factions living in the area. He left Mecca under the cover of darkness and made the journey with a small group of followers. Although they sometimes experienced problems with their new neighbors, in this environment the Muslim community was able to grow and develop without the tensions that confronted them in Mecca. Muhammad spent the rest of his life in Yathrib, where he is buried. It became so closely identified with him that its name was changed to *madinat al-nabi* ("city of the prophet"), which is usually shortened to Medina ("city").

Muhammad's final task was to convert his hometown of Mecca to the new religion of Islam. After a number of pilgrimages to the city, he was eventually able to win over the leading citizens of the city, and the rest of the population soon followed. The story of how he entered Mecca and transformed the Kaaba into a shrine commemorating worship of the only God is one of the most celebrated traditions in Islamic lore. By the time Muhammad died in 632, Islam was present throughout the entire Arabian Peninsula and was poised to spread throughout much of the known world.

## 2. What are the main subgroups within the religion?

*Judaism.*    Probably nowhere is the diversity of contemporary Judaism more sharply clarified than in the classification devised by Leo Trepp.[1] There he explains the variety of interpretations of Judaism at the dawn of the twentieth century in terms of six different groups. The first he titles "Old Orthodoxy," which taught that the Torah is divine and must be obeyed without question. Judaism exists by itself without contact with the outside world, which is seen as invariably hostile. This form of orthodoxy, which is still practiced in some circles and which rejects any hint of change, prevailed pri-

---

1. See Leo Trepp, *A History of the Jewish Experience: Eternal Faith, Eternal People* (New York: Behrman House, 1962), 314–15.

marily in Eastern Europe. It still persists, however, in certain communities around the world. One explanation for such rigid discipline in the past was that the performance of the commandments in all their minute details was a psychological defense mechanism against the intolerable hardships of persecution. It gave the people great strength through strict observance, while the expectation of a personal messiah provided them with much-needed hope of relief from their hardships.

A second form of Jewish faith in our time is neo-Orthodoxy. For followers of this modern discipline, the Torah is divine and obedience to it is a service to humankind. The concept of the chosen people implies that the Jews everywhere must set a moral standard for all to emulate. Secular culture contains wisdom worth seeking; adjustment to the modern world is essential but may not conflict with the observance of Torah. Good citizenship is a supreme religious obligation. Aesthetic values too can be ennobling and uplifting.

For Conservative Judaism the divinity of Torah is grounded in the consent of the people. The community itself with the passage of time will adjust its commandments to their needs. Major emphasis is directed to history so that the past is a primary guide to inform the future. Acceptance of new knowledge and observance depends on the will of the people. Zionism is a central precept because of the spiritual and national bonds it signifies for the Jewish people. Aesthetic values too are important for uniting and elevating the community.

Reform Judaism strives to maintain a balance between change and continuity. Some directions it pursues are familiar; others, less so; but in every instance it offers a vision of the Covenant that is constantly evolving and is never static. In spite of its changing character, however, certain essential principles remain firm at any given period. The first is the freedom of any generation to examine existing practice and to change it for sound and sufficient reasons. In addition, Reform emphasizes the right to modify public worship for the purpose of enriching the experience of communal prayer. And finally, a dominant principle of Reform has been its emphasis on the mission of social justice inherent in our biblical legacy. This stress on right conduct as the path to human fulfillment is perhaps the precept in Judaism most central to Reform.

In America today, and throughout most of the Western world, Jews are divided principally into those three major branches—Orthodox, Conservative, and Reform. The differences among them revolve more often around matters of ritual observance than of theological belief. Orthodox Jews adhere to Judaism as they believe it was conceived in Talmudic times with as little accommodation as possible to competing systems of truth and knowledge. Reform Judaism assigns high priority to blending the ancient heritage with the teachings of modern science and humanities. Conservative Judaism stands generally between these two, retaining as much of traditional learning as possible while also embracing contemporary civilization.

Worship in the Orthodox synagogue is entirely in Hebrew; men and women sit separately; head coverings are mandatory for men as a sign of reverence and respect for God. The Conservative service is somewhat shorter and conducted about equally in Hebrew and English. Head coverings are customary, but men and women usually sit together.

Reform Jewish worship is even more abbreviated, although its newest prayer book permits a lengthier service. The liturgy usually consists of more English than Hebrew, and head coverings are optional. Men and women are always seated together, and instrumental music is a customary fixture.

Orthodox Judaism requires the observance of dietary laws as the Bible prescribes and the Talmud amplifies, the so-called laws of *kashrut*. Those laws include the prohibition of certain foods, the proper slaughtering of animals for human consumption, and a ban on consuming meat and dairy foods during the same meal. Theoretically, Conservative Jews are obligated to observe these same dietary laws, though more often than not their observance is inconsistent. Although in recent years a small segment of Reform Jews have begun observing dietary laws, the vast majority still do not.

The current distinctions among these movements are often blurred. While differences between Orthodoxy and Reform are readily apparent, the range of ritual and ceremonial practice within each branch makes it difficult to detect distinctive divisions. None of them is monolithic. Some Orthodox Jews are fanatically opposed to all change while others are more moderate, recognizing that some flexibility is necessary. Conservative Jews may lean either toward Orthodoxy or Reform.

Within Reform too there are significant differences. One group insists that Reform Judaism must remain what it was in the nineteenth and early twentieth centuries, with primary emphasis on social justice and the ethical mandates of prophetic Judaism. A much larger number are convinced that, like all movements of protest, Reform began as a revolution but must now achieve a more reasonable and moderate stance. Most Reform Jews today are far more supportive of traditional ritual and Hebrew language than were their predecessors. Jewish observance, in short, covers a wide spectrum of activity within every movement from the most traditional to the most progressive.

An additional group of Jews in America have created a fourth branch that they call Reconstructionism. This option was founded by Rabbi Mordecai Kaplan in the early twentieth century and attempted to bridge the distance between Conservative and Reform Judaism. Its most distinctive attribute is their emphasis on Judaism as a religious civilization rather than exclusively a religious faith. It also assigns high priority to the role of Israel for Jews and Jewish life everywhere, and has infused Jewish religious thought with elements of naturalism.

Whatever adjectives may divide the Jewish people, much more unites them. Believers and nonbelievers, religionists and secularists, all of them are part of the same Jewish people. One of the most fundamental concepts in Jewish life is *k'lal yisrael*—the community or totality of the Jewish people. Except for a small fanatical fringe, all Jews, regardless of their differences, recognize that the whole is greater than the sum of its parts and that they belong, with diverse interpretations of deity and destiny, to a single entity—the Jewish people. Nothing matters more.

*Christianity.*    Approximately one-third of the world's population, nearly two billion people, regard themselves as Christian, and their faith traditions are almost innumerably diverse. In spite of that diversity, we can identify three main subgroups: Eastern Orthodoxy, Roman Catholicism, and Protestantism. Each subgroup emerged and developed within a particular historical and cultural setting that accounts in part for its cohesiveness.

Eastern Orthodoxy and Roman Catholicism emerged from the experiences of the earliest church, but they began to develop distinct emphases very early. In spite of efforts to affirm and maintain the unity of the Christian church, as Christianity spread across the Roman Empire during its first thousand years, it developed a division that fell along linguistic lines: Latin in the West, and Greek in the East. The Western church developed into Roman Catholicism, and the Eastern church developed into the Eastern Orthodox communions. In the East, the cities of Alexandria in Egypt, Antioch in Syria, Constantinople in modern-day Turkey, and, to a lesser extent, Jerusalem, rose to prominence, and the bishops of those cities became known as patriarchs. In the West, however, the bishop of Rome—later known as the pope—stood without equal. The bishop of Rome understood himself to hold primacy over all other bishops, but the patriarchs rejected this claim of primacy. The question of the relative authority of the bishop of Rome stood near the center of every controversy between East and West, and eventually became part of the reason that the Roman Catholic Church and the churches of the East officially separated, each refusing to recognize the authority of the other.

Beyond the dispute about the authority of the pope, this division between the Eastern and Western churches was almost inevitable given cultural differences characteristic of the Greek and Latin traditions as well as political developments in the fourth and fifth centuries. The traditions of the Latin-speaking portion of the empire, even before Christianity, had always been more focused on the practical and legal than had the Greek-speaking East, which tended to be more philosophical and even mystical. It has sometimes been noted that the Romans built roads and the Greeks built philosophical systems! The contours of belief in the East were essentially established through a series of controversies that were addressed at councils in the fourth and fifth centuries. These controversies focused on questions about the Trinity and on the nature of the relationship between humanity and divinity in Christ. Those emphases continue to characterize Eastern Orthodoxy today. In the West, controversies tended to revolve around questions about whether human beings contribute to their salvation, the nature of church authority, and how the church and state ought to be related to one another.

An important political development also contributed to the different ways in which Eastern Orthodoxy and Roman Catholicism developed. By the early fifth century the western half of the empire had begun to disintegrate in the face of increasing "barbarian" invasions. As the structures of civilization in the West began to crumble, the church increasingly had to take on the role of governing authority in both temporal and spiritual matters. This meant that the church based in Rome had to focus on practical and even legal concerns as much as it did on the spiritual well-being of those in its care. But in the East, the empire remained intact—as did the basic infrastructure of civilization—all the way into the modern period, even when it came under the governance of the Muslims in the fifteenth century.

In spite of these differences, Roman Catholicism and Eastern Orthodoxy have much in common that distinguishes them from Protestant Christianity. For instance, they share an understanding of the church as the continuation of apostolic tradition and especially value the authority of bishops as the successors to the apostles. The tradition of faith, in both Roman Catholicism and Eastern Orthodoxy, carries enormous authority in matters of belief and practice. Both traditions have developed monastic communities whose members are devoted to striving for perfection in Christian living. And both Roman Catholicism and Eastern Orthodoxy teach that salvation requires the grace of God to be met by human effort and response.

In the sixteenth century a further division developed in the church in Europe when a series of reform movements led some—called the Protestants—to reject the authority of the Roman Catholic Church and to form their own church traditions and authority structures. The Protestants wanted to reform both belief and practice in the church. They rejected the authority of the pope and taught that individual Christians did not require a priest to mediate between themselves and God. They taught that no one could merit salvation, which could be received only as a free gift from God. They insisted that the Bible alone carried final authority for Christians. They also challenged long-established practices such as the veneration of saints, the use of images and statuary in the worship space, and the use of Latin in worship and as the language of the Bible—a language that most sixteenth-century Europeans no longer understood. They translated the Bible into local languages such as German and English. They also permitted clergy to marry, something prohibited in the Roman Catholic Church but permitted of Eastern Orthodox priests. Instead of founding a single, new church, Protestant communities developed somewhat independently under the influence of different reformers, such as Martin Luther, Ulrich Zwingli, and John Calvin, and eventually differentiated themselves into denominations such as Methodist, Episcopal, Baptist, Presbyterian, and Lutheran as well as into myriad independent congregations.

*Islam.*   There is a strong sense of unity and solidarity among Muslims that goes all the way back to the earliest days of the religion. When Muhammad introduced Islam into Arabia he simultaneously brought about a change in how the people of the area would identify and align themselves. It had been a tribal-based society for centuries, which meant people looked first to their tribe for identity and protection. For example, Muhammad's family was a member of the Hashem clan, which was part of the powerful Quraysh tribe that played an influential role in Arabian society. With the rise of Islam such alliances that were formed along tribal and familial lines were called into question. The important thing became membership in the Muslim community, not affiliation with a particular tribe or clan. The Arabic term that was adopted to designate this faith-based group was *ummah*, and it is still commonly used to refer to the worldwide Islamic community to which all Muslims pledge their allegiance.

This is not to say there are no divisions within Islam. Muslims differentiate themselves in all sorts of social, cultural, and ideological ways. Despite those distinctions they still recognize each other as fellow believers and members of the one *ummah*. The most well-known division in Islam is that between Sunni and Shia Muslims. To understand the origin and reasons for this split we need to return back to seventh-century Arabia.

When Muhammad died in 632, the overriding concern for the young Muslim community was who would take his place. He had not appointed a successor, and there was no system in place to ensure a smooth transition of authority. One group wanted a man named Ali, who was the Prophet's cousin and son-in-law, to become the new leader. They reasoned it would be important to keep control within Muhammad's family, and Ali was the perfect candidate. Others thought differently and felt the new leader should be someone who knew the Prophet personally, regardless of whether or not he was a relative.

The latter group eventually won out. A series of three different companions of Muhammad were appointed leader before Ali assumed the office of caliph ("successor") and held it until his death in 661. This period of Islamic history is referred to as the time of the four "Rightly Guided Caliphs." When Ali died, his followers believed the caliphate would be kept in his family line, but the majority group passed over his sons in favor of a man named Muawiya, whose reign ushered in the Umayyad Period (661–750).

Those who backed Ali in these battles over authority called themselves *shia*, from an Arabic word meaning "partisans" that gave a name to the movement. Shia Muslims are those of the "party of Ali" who believe the leaders of the *ummah* throughout history should have been taken from among his descendants. Today they number about 15 percent of all Muslims. They consider themselves to be a persecuted minority that has been denied its rightful place, but they believe they will eventually be vindicated and all Muslims will come under the authority of someone from Ali's line. This is a topic to which we will return in the chapter on leadership.

With some relatively minor exceptions that will be discussed later, the beliefs and practices of Sunnis and Shia closely mirror each other. They each consider the other to be legitimate expressions of Islam, and each deems the followers of the other sect to be fellow Muslims. In recent history there have been some violent clashes between Sunnis and Shia, as in the Iran-Iraq War of the 1980s, but these are usually based on political disagreements rather than theological differences.

With only two main branches of division, Islam lacks the diversity and variety of a religion like Christianity, which contains many factions and denominations. There are a number of other Islamic groups whose names are familiar to non-Muslims, but they are more like offshoots of Islam rather than major branches within it. One is Wahhabi Islam, a radical form of the faith found primarily in modern Saudi Arabia that traces its roots back to a man named Muhammad Ibn Abd al-Wahhab (1703–92). With the endorsement of the powerful Saud family, he was able to spread his extreme brand of the faith throughout the Arabian Peninsula. He thought Islam had been tainted by improper innovations and corrupt practices, and he went about the task of trying to remove these elements from it. Osama bin Laden and his supporters are the most notorious adherents of Wahhabism.

Another group that is well-known in the United States is the Nation of Islam. It was founded in the 1930s by a man named Fard as an organization that attempted to respond to the needs and concerns of African Americans.

Elijah Muhammad took over the reins after Fard's mysterious disappearance, and under his leadership the Nation of Islam came to wield a great deal of religious and social influence in many American cities. Because of certain teachings that run counter to mainstream Islam its relationship with the rest of the *ummah* has been problematic. For example, the Nation of Islam maintains that Fard was God incarnate and that Elijah Muhammad was a prophet, two beliefs that no Sunni or Shia would be able to accept. In recent years, Elijah Muhammad's successor Louis Farrakhan has attempted to reach out to the worldwide Islamic community and improve relations with other Muslims.

## 3. Where is the religion found today?

*Judaism.*    The major centers of Jewish life today consist of American Jewry and Israel. Of the nearly fourteen million Jews in the world today, roughly eleven million live in these two countries alone, approximately five million in the United States and six million in Israel. Viable but smaller Jewish communities may also be found in Canada, Great Britain, France, South Africa, Australia, and certain countries in South America.

Prior to World War II most Jews lived in Western or Eastern Europe. Their total number approached nine million. In executing the Final Solution, however, the Nazis destroyed nearly six million of them. As a consequence, nearly two out of every three Jews in Europe perished in the Holocaust, and the basic foundations of Jewish life that had existed from the days of the Roman Empire came to a catastrophic end.

Quite remarkably, however, the revival of Jewish life and Jewish communities in recent years in the lands of the former Soviet Union is as astounding as it is encouraging. Both Orthodoxy under the auspices of the Lubavitch movement and Reform Judaism supported by the World Union for Progressive Judaism have reopened old synagogues, built new ones, and sparked a new interest in Jewish learning and culture. The results have been most impressive in relatively little time.

In defining their Jewishness, American Jews generally attach high priority to moral responsibility and to the inner life of the spirit. Most of them are not necessarily pious in their religious observance and may not even attend synagogue regularly, but they believe deeply in supporting basic Jewish ideals of helping the poor and disadvantaged, pursuing justice and equality for all peoples, revering the sanctity of life, supporting quality education, and advancing worthy philanthropic causes as a religious obligation rather than an occasional momentary impulse.

Another crucial factor in American Jewish identity is a commitment to Jewish sovereignty and the state of Israel. Many are convinced that the future security of Jewish life anywhere depends on the existence of an independent Jewish state. The argument contends that had there been such a place for the Jews of Europe prior to the Holocaust, the outcome may have been far less horrendous.

Israeli Jews ironically are much less religiously observant than their peers in other countries. The focus of Jewish life elsewhere is primarily religious, but in Israel the prevailing emphasis is cultural. To be sure, Israel includes a wide range of pious Orthodox sects that in recent years have grown significantly in political as well as spiritual influence, but the vast majority of Israelis are still largely secular. Most do not attend synagogues or observe standard rituals or ceremonies with any regularity. They will observe only major holy days such as Yom Kippur (the Day of Atonement) or Passover, and even those with only perfunctory regard for their religious significance.

Israel grants religious freedom to all faith communities under its jurisdiction. Christians and Muslims govern their own institutions and manage their own affairs. In the Jewish sector, however, the Ministry of Religion delegates authority for all religious matters to the Chief Rabbinate, which consists of both an Ashkenazic chief rabbi and a Sephardic chief rabbi, with an extensive administrative entourage for each. Neither religious authority will recognize the prerogative of any Reform or Conservative clergy in matters of personal status, such as conversion, marriage, and divorce. The struggle for equal recognition of all branches of Judaism in Israel is an ongoing legal struggle that in recent years has achieved significant progress.

Regardless of religious disagreements, however, Jews in Israel and those outside are inseparably linked through bonds of *am'cha*—peoplehood. Wherever Jews may live they are firmly united by a common, collective past and an equally firm determination to complete their mission as an *ohr lagoyim*, "a light unto the nations."

*Christianity.*    Christianity has spread across every region of the globe. At first it grew and flourished primarily in regions that belonged to the Roman Empire: Europe, the Near East, and North Africa. During the medieval period (500–1500), Roman Catholicism spread into Western Europe, while Eastern Orthodoxy spread into Russia and the Slavic nations. At the same time, most in the Near East and North Africa converted to Islam. The third main subgroup, Protestantism, emerged in Europe in the sixteenth century and spread, as did Roman Catholicism, wherever European colonialism spread during the modern period.

For this reason, it is easy to imagine Christianity to be a phenomenon of the western and northern hemispheres, a faith tradition for Europeans and North Americans of European ancestry. But the Christian faith has always been remarkably adaptable. Africans brought to North America as slaves, for example, fused a newfound faith with their own cultural traditions to shape a distinctive African American expression of Christianity that persists even today. The twentieth and twenty-first centuries have seen the rapid growth of Christian faith traditions rooted in indigenous cultures beyond Europe and North America. The growth of Christianity in the emerging world represents not so much an official break with Eastern Orthodoxy, Roman Catholicism, or European/North American Protestantism as it does a response and adaptation of the faith to cultural contexts very different from the ones in which those traditions developed, including experiences of colonialism and of marginalization by economic structures that privilege industrialized nations.

We can gain a sense of the reach of the Christian faith by drawing on statistics gleaned from the World Christian Database.[2] In places like Europe, Latin America, North America, and Oceania, Christianity dominates the religious scene. Seventy-six percent of Europeans, for example, and 93 percent of Latin Americans identify themselves as Christian. In North America the figure reaches 83 percent, with 80 percent of the residents of Oceania affirming the Christian faith. In Africa, nearly half of the population, 46 percent, is Christian. In Asia, less than 10 percent of the population is Christian; even so, numerically, there are more Christians in Asia, nearly 351 million, than there are in North America, which has about 277 million. There are also more Christians in Africa (411 million) than there are in North America. Likewise, in spite of the perception of Christianity as a religion of the northern hemisphere, and in spite of its much longer historical presence in Europe, there are nearly as many Christians in Latin America (517 million) as there are in Europe (553 million).

The Christian faith, then, is both broadly and deeply diverse. There is more than merely a scattering of Christians outside of Europe and North America. In fact, the majority of Christians live outside of those regions. In recent decades, leaders in Christian denominations in North America and Europe have become increasingly aware of the breadth and diversity of Christian traditions outside of the North and West, and have become appreciative especially of how worship practices that emerge in different contexts might enrich and correct their own traditions. As a result, it is no longer unusual to find a

---

2. The World Christian Database is a repository of population statistics related to religion that is sponsored by the Center for the Study of Global Christianity at Gordon-Conwell Theological Seminary. The database is available online at www.worldchristiandatabase.org.

congregation in middle America singing a hymn to a traditional African folk melody or offering a prayer composed by a Latin American priest.

*Islam.* By the end of the period of the Rightly Guided Caliphs in 661, Islam had experienced remarkable growth and expansion. From its relatively humble beginnings in Arabia it quickly spread westward across North Africa, northward into the area of modern-day Israel, Lebanon, and Syria, and westward as far as India. The reasons for that rapid development are many and varied, but one of the most important was the strategy the Muslim empire adopted as it entered non-Muslim territories.

Many non-Muslims assume that Islam spread through violent and hostile means, but this was not actually the case. Rather, the Muslim forces gave local populations a choice upon entering their lands. They first invited them to convert to Islam and become part of the *ummah*, which some chose to do. Those who preferred not to become Muslims and were followers of one of the other monotheistic religions were allowed to continue to practice their faith as long as they paid an extra tax, which gave them the status of protected minorities. Many chose this option because the Muslim authorities, unlike the Byzantines who preceded them, adopted a hands-off policy toward those living in areas under their control. Non-Muslims were given a great deal of independence and freedom under Islam, and so, ironically, Christians fared better under Muslim rule than they did under their fellow Christians the Byzantines, who tended to meddle more in the affairs of their subjects. Only if neither of these options was taken—which was a very rare occurrence—would the Muslim forces engage in military battle with non-Muslims.

That approach toward expansion was abandoned a long time ago, but throughout the centuries Islam has continued to spread. Muslims are now found in virtually every country in the world, and it is the fastest-growing religion on the planet. The worldwide Muslim population exceeds one billion people, which means that approximately one of every five people on the face of the earth is a Muslim.

It is therefore wrong to equate Islam with the Middle East, a mistake made by many non-Muslims. Arabs comprise only about 15 percent of the total Muslim population. In fact, only one Arab country (Egypt) makes the list of the top ten most heavily populated Muslim nations, and it comes in at number nine. The first five on that list—Indonesia, India, Pakistan, Bangladesh, and China—are all quite far removed from the Middle East, the part of the world that is often associated with Islam.

Shia Islam is found throughout the world, but the country that has the largest number and largest percentage of Shia Muslims is Iran, where about

95 percent of its 75 million people follow that branch of the faith. Iraq and Lebanon are two other countries in which Shia Islam has played an important and influential role.

Islam has had a more visible presence in the Western world in recent decades as a result of increased Muslim immigration to non-Muslim lands, marriages between Muslims and non-Muslims, and conversions to the faith. Because the U.S. Census Bureau does not collect information on religious affiliation, the exact number of Muslims in the United States is not known, but most estimates put the total at somewhere between five and ten million. While a significant proportion of America's Muslims live in large cities, they can be found throughout the country. For example, many people are quite surprised to learn that the oldest mosque in the United States is located in Cedar Rapids, Iowa. Similarly, the headquarters of the Islamic Society of North America, the largest organization in the country that addresses the interests and concerns of North American Muslims, is located in Plainfield, Indiana.

Chapter Two

# Dates, People, and Places

## 1. What were the most significant events in the history of the religion?

*Judaism.*   Jewish history spans a range of four thousand years. It is obviously difficult to single out over that vast period of time only a handful of people, places, and events that deserve special recognition. Every century, indeed every generation, triggered decisive turning points that forever altered the direction of Jewish life and faith.

The first and most notable such signpost is the fact that, of all the religions in the world, only Judaism designed its calendar based not on any major event or personality in its own history but on a moment of universal application. That moment was the creation of the world according to biblical calculation. Judaism does not measure time from the birth of Abraham, or the exodus from Egypt, or the revelation at Sinai, but from the theoretical beginning of the universe, which precedes any particular Jewish experience.

The history of Judaism itself may be easier to digest if it is framed in terms of antiquity, medieval times, and the modern world. Antiquity ranges from earliest prehistoric beginnings in biblical narrative to the close of the Talmudic period in the seventh century CE. That span of nearly twenty-five hundred years starts with the patriarchs Abraham, Isaac, and Jacob and continues with the advent of Moses and the subsequent liberation from Egyptian bondage (probably in the thirteenth century BCE) and the eventual entry into Canaan under the rule of the Judges.

By the tenth century BCE the people prevailed upon the priesthood to sanction the formation of a monarchy, first under Saul, then under David and Solomon. Because of political intrigue and internal rebellion following the death of Solomon, the monarchy split into a northern kingdom of Israel and a southern kingdom of Judah. The former fell to the Assyrian Empire in 722

BCE while Judah survived until its conquest by the Babylonians in 586 BCE. The restoration of sovereignty and a second commonwealth under the Hasmoneans in the second century BCE eventually ended in disaster in 70 AD when the Roman Empire crushed every last vestige of independence for the Jewish people. A sovereign Jewish nation would not revive again for two thousand years until the rebirth of Israel in 1948.

The distinctive character of the Jewish people, however, would blossom not in political or military power but in spiritual and cultural greatness. In addition to the scriptural text called the Written Law, rabbinic teaching added its own interpretations called the Oral Law. The first codification of such commentaries following the canonization of the Bible in the third century BCE, for example, culminated in a voluminous work called the Mishnah, edited in the third century CE by the leading rabbinic sage of his time, Rabbi Judah the Prince.

Nearly three hundred years later an additional extensive collection of commentaries (Gemara) was collected and together with the Mishnah was called the Talmud. In traditional Jewish circles, this encyclopedia of Jewish law and lore remains to the present day the definitive document for understanding Jewish belief and practice.

The medieval period witnessed two divergent paths in Jewish history. Jewish communities in northern Europe came to be known as Ashkenazim, because they originated in Germany, called Ashkenaz in Hebrew. Jews who lived around the Mediterranean basin from the Near East to North Africa and southern Europe called themselves Sephardim, a derivation of the Hebrew word for Spain, Sephard.

Throughout the Middle Ages the Talmud served as the primary source of authority for Jewish belief and practice for both Ashkenazim and Sephardim. The only digression from that circumstance was the emergence of Karaism in the eighth century CE, which lasted until well into the fifteenth century CE. This revolt against the authority of rabbinic law in the Talmud was so ominous that during the Reformation Catholics often hurled the epithet "Karaites" at Protestants as a derogatory epithet. Karaism taught that the kingdom of God as revealed in the Torah was imminent and that the observance of the Oral Law (the Talmud) was no longer necessary. The difficulty, of course, was that rejection of rabbinic authority in the eighth century CE was a lot easier than living literally by the provisions of the Torah that originated in the twelfth century BCE.

Like the earlier teachers of the Mishnah, the more enlightened and realistic Karaite scholars began to develop an "oral law" of their own, disguised as expansions of the biblical text. The movement eventually lapsed into anarchy and, after surviving in isolated regions for a limited time, eventually faltered and disappeared.

The Karaitic revolt, however, served a useful purpose. It prevented Talmudism from becoming static at this point of its history. It forced Jewish law to come to terms with the realities of its own time instead of remaining paralyzed in an ancient legal system. It taught Jews that creative survival lies neither in absolute freedom nor absolute conformity, but in a calculated blend of both.

*Christianity.*    The events of the life, death, and resurrection of Christ are the most important in the history of Christianity. They set the founding narrative through which the rest of history is interpreted by Christians. Beyond these events, however, we can identify several crucial moments that have shaped the Christian faith. First among these is the destruction of the Temple in Jerusalem in the year 70 following a Jewish rebellion against the Roman Empire. That event marked the beginning of the period of persecution and the end of the period in which Christianity was considered a sect within Judaism. The martyrs who died for their faith in the face of persecution were raised up as heroes, and the *lapsi* who recanted their faith in the face of persecution, and who subsequently sought forgiveness and readmission to the church, forced the church to think carefully about the nature of forgiveness and about who may receive and administer the sacraments. The separation from Judaism, along with the emergence of competing groups claiming the name "Christian" for themselves, prompted the church to identify which of the writings in circulation among the Christian churches were authentic Scripture and to form the New Testament to be read as Scripture together with the Hebrew Bible. This process of identifying which writings are Scripture is known as "canon formation," and it took several centuries. Not until the year 367 do we find a public list of documents that are considered part of the New Testament that matches precisely what is in use today.

A second crucial event in shaping the Christian religion is the conversion of the emperor Constantine and the theological and doctrinal developments that followed in its wake, especially the formulation of the Nicene Creed in 325. That creed set boundaries on what Christians may and may not believe, and was crucial for ensuring some measure of unity amid the diversity of Christian belief. The Nicene Creed made it a point of orthodoxy that Jesus Christ is both fully human (a point contested by a group called the Gnostics, and later by a theologian named Apollinaris) and fully divine (a point contested by a theologian named Arius). The council also established a precedent for calling ecumenical councils (meetings of the worldwide church) to decide matters of orthodoxy, matters that go to the heart of what it means to be Christian. The alignment of the church with the power of the Roman Empire opened an important opportunity for the faith to spread and flourish, but it also opened the church to the danger that it may simply come to endorse the prevailing culture. And, indeed, we see this mixed heritage in the history of Christianity: at times, Christians have used their positions of power to advocate for justice, but at other times they have simply substituted the values of the powerful for the values of the gospel.

The schism between the Eastern and Western churches constitutes a third important event in the history of Christianity, though it really is a series of events. The schism can be traced throughout the history of the church, beginning with the collapse of the western half of the Roman Empire in the fifth century, continuing through a number of disagreements about the jurisdiction and authority of the pope, and culminating in 1204 when Western Christians participating in the fourth crusade sacked the holiest church in the East, the Hagia Sophia. The schism has meant that the church has been unable to call an ecumenical council since the eighth century. With the founding of the World Council of Churches in 1948, we find Christians once again seeking ways to restore full communion among all Christians while also honoring the deep diversity that has always marked the Christian faith.

A fourth important event, the Protestant Reformation, brought sweeping theological and liturgical changes in European Christianity. Reformers translated the Bible into vernacular languages, emphasized the centrality of preaching in worship, permitted clergy to marry, encouraged individual Christians to read and interpret the Bible, and questioned the authority of tradition. The Reformation also had important political consequences. After the collapse of the Roman Empire in the West, Europe entered a period when the church had represented the only centralized source of authority. To be Roman Catholic and to be European, a subject of the Holy Roman Empire, were virtually synonymous. We sometimes refer to this fusion of religion and culture during the medieval period as Christendom. With the emergence of Protestantism, we find a fracturing of Christendom that coincided with the emergence of independent European nations in the place of the vision of a unified Holy Roman Empire in the West. In addition, because Protestantism challenged the hierarchy between priests and people, it opened the door to democratic movements that challenged the hierarchy between kings and subjects.

The Second Vatican Council (1962–65) represents a fifth important event in the history of Christianity. At this council, the Roman Catholic Church entered a new period of what was called "openness," in which it acknowledged the faithfulness of Protestants as "separated brethren," granted permission for worship services to be conducted in local languages rather than the traditional Latin, committed itself to increased lay involvement in worship leadership, affirmed the presence of truth in non-Christian religions, and condemned anti-Semitism.

*Islam.*    Key episodes of Muhammad's life are recalled and celebrated by Muslims as important moments in the history of their community. According to Islamic tradition, Muhammad began to receive the revelations that eventually came to comprise the Qur'an during the month of Ramadan in the year 610. The "Night of Power," which commemorates that event, is one of the holiest times of the Muslim calendar and is celebrated with great solemnity every year during the month of fasting. There is a difference of opinion regarding exactly what day of the month the revelations commenced, but most place it somewhere during the last ten days of Ramadan.

Muslims consider the *hijra*, the journey from Mecca to Medina that Muhammad made with a small group of followers, to be the most significant event in the early history of Islam. It was this change of location that allowed the nascent Muslim community to survive and develop into the influential religion it has become. The journey is so highly regarded that it was taken as the founding experience of the *ummah* that gave birth to Islam. For this reason, the year 622 is considered to be the start of the Muslim calendar, which is now in the first half of the fifteenth century. Islam uses a lunar calendar, which is a bit shorter than the solar one found in the West, so one cannot determine the year of the Muslim calendar simply by deducting 622 from its Western counterpart. Dates in the Muslim calendar are often written with the initials AH after them, which is an abbreviation of the Latin term *anno hegirae*, "in the year of the *hijra*."

Another celebrated event of the prophet's life has its basis in Qur'an 17:1, which speaks of God transporting "His servant from the sacred mosque to the furthest mosque." Muslim interpretations have understood this passage to be a reference to Muhammad and a miraculous night journey he made from Mecca (the location of the "sacred mosque") to Jerusalem, where the "furthest mosque" (*al-aqsa* in Arabic) is found. According to this tradition Muhammad was then taken up through the various levels of heaven, where he was welcomed and honored by many of the great prophets of the past. This event has been frequently depicted in art, and some Muslim mystics, or Sufis, have understood it to be a metaphor of the soul's journey to God.

Muhammad's birth and death have sometimes been celebrated by Muslims, but this practice has never caught on in the community as a whole. In fact, in some periods and places Muslims have been forbidden from commemorating the beginning and end of the prophet's life. This prohibition is often expressed in theological terms—Muhammad was only a man like all of the prophets, and so he deserves no special treatment or recognition. Some Muslim thinkers have voiced concern that such observances run the risk of divinizing Muhammad in a way similar to what has happened with Jesus in Christian celebrations of his birth and resurrection at Christmas and Easter.

A very important moment in Shia history occurred in 680, when Ali's son Husayn was killed by Sunni forces at a place called Karbala in modern-day Iraq. Husayn and his followers were on their way to Damascus to claim the leadership of the Muslim community that they believed was rightfully his when they were attacked and brutally slain by their enemies. This tragic event is recalled each year by Shia Muslims, who mourn the martyrdom of Husayn and reenact the circumstances of his death in a ritual passion play known as the ta'ziya.

The classical period of Islam came to an end in 1258, when Mongols invaded from the East and captured the city of Baghdad, which had served as the capital of the Muslim empire throughout the Abassid Period (750–1258). This was a significant event not just because it signaled the official end of the caliphate form of government that had begun with the death of Muhammad in 632. It also began a process of debate over who can legitimately rule Muslims. The Mongols converted to Islam, but because they were outsiders some believed they were unfit to govern the *ummah*. This is an issue that has continued to be discussed in the modern day because some Muslim extremists, like Osama bin Laden, maintain they have the right to oust from office those leaders they deem to be not "Muslim" enough.

In modern times, the Iranian Revolution of 1979 was a watershed event for many Muslims. Under the leadership of Ayatollah Khomeini the people of Iran were able to overthrow the Shah, a longtime ally of the United States who had relegated Islam to a marginal role in society. This marked the first time an Islamic regime had been able to replace a more secular form of government, a development that gave much hope to those who think this model should be adopted throughout the Muslim world. More than a quarter-century later, the Islamic Republic of Iran still plays a pivotal role in the international community.

## 2. Who have been the key people in the development of the religion?

*Judaism.* Most of the key people in Jewish biblical narrative are familiar to Christians and Muslims as well as Jews. Abraham, Isaac, and Jacob and their families founded and followed a faith rooted in covenant with an invisible god they believed to be more powerful than any other. The greatest of all prophets, Moses, supposedly elevated this belief into the concept of ethical monotheism, but more likely that ideal did not fully emerge until the period of the later prophets.

Saul is distinguished as the first king of Israel who achieved Jewish sovereignty over the land stipulated in Israel's sacred covenant. King David established Jerusalem as the capital of the country, and Solomon, of course, built the Temple in Jerusalem as the central shrine for the entire nation.

During the Talmudic period, any number of heroes and sages could be cited for their lasting contribution to Jewish learning and history. The most notable were probably Judah the Prince, who in the third century CE edited the Mishnah, and Rav Ashi and Ravina, who completed the Talmud about two hundred years later. Certainly the story of Chanukah, the first struggle for religious freedom against the Greek-Syrian Empire in 168 BCE, could not be told without the legendary leadership of Mattathias the Maccabee and later his son Judah and his supporters.

Understanding medieval Jewry requires an awareness of the two major communities in the Jewish world at that time, which were mentioned earlier. Although Ashkenazim and Sephardim adhered to similar precepts of faith, they often differed sharply in their ritual and ceremonial observance and even in their particular priorities for study and learning. Ashkenazi Jews concentrated mostly on Talmudic discourse and its continuing application to Jewish life. Scholars who were the major exponents of this discipline included the great commentator Rashi in the eleventh century in France and Joseph Karo in the sixteenth century, who was the author of the *Shulchan Aruk,* the most authoritative code of Jewish observance. Karo was actually by birth a Sephardic Jew, a fact that originally evoked enormous opposition to his pronouncements among Ashkenazim until a Polish scholar named Moses Isserles later added footnotes reflecting the Ashkenazi interpretation of his work.

Meanwhile, among medieval Sephardic Jewry, learning was not limited to Jewish texts but extended into the larger world of Islamic culture. The Jews of Spain enjoyed much greater freedom and latitude than did their peers in Europe, who were confined to ghettos, deprived of dignity, and subject to the whims of Christian rulers and clergy.

Jewish learning in Sephardic lands emphasized studies in philosophy, poetry, mathematics, and astronomy. Its leading luminaries included Saadia Gaon in the tenth century, Solomon ibn Gabirol and Judah Halevi in the eleventh, and perhaps the greatest Jewish philosopher of any generation, Moses Maimonides in the twelfth century, whose major work, *The Guide for the Perplexed*, remains the crowning achievement of Jewish belief and thought. Jews under Islamic rule, in spite of certain forms of discrimination as a religious minority, clearly enjoyed much greater political, economic, and social status than in Christian Europe.

Jewish life in the Ashkenazi world began its decline with the inception of the Crusades in 1096 CE. The status of Jews in Christian Europe, despite occasional brief periods of recovery, deteriorated steadily after that time with increasingly dire consequences. Among Sephardic Jews the "Golden Age" ended essentially in the thirteenth century and culminated in 1492 with the expulsion of Jews from Spain and later from Portugal in 1496. Most Sephardic Jews later migrated to Turkey, Holland, the New World, and other non-Catholic countries.

In the late eighteenth century a movement of Jewish spiritual revival emerged in Eastern Europe founded by Israel of Moldavia, better known as the Baal Shem Tov. He was in the truest sense a religious revivalist, and the sect he founded, known as Hasidism ("the pious ones") depended as much on his radiant personality as on his teachings. Hasidism substituted a warm mysticism for the arid scholasticism that it attacked. It emphasized service to God through joy and celebration even more than learning and scholarship. Its basic concept was the omnipresence of God in all the universe, in mind and in matter, in every relationship, in evil as in good.

The modern world in Jewish terms opens most visibly with the period of Enlightenment in the eighteenth century and more specifically with the emancipation of European Jewry under Napoleon in the early nineteenth century. Jewish communities in Western Europe enjoyed, at least for a brief period, newfound political, economic, and social equality under the banner of Napoleonic reform. Eventually, with the restoration of the former monarchies, those benefits gradually dissipated and dissolved. Jews in Eastern Europe fared even worse until brutal Czarist pogroms sparked massive waves of emigration to America in the late nineteenth century.

In 1897 Dr. Theodor Herzl, a Viennese journalist and social critic, convened a gathering in Basel, Switzerland, called the Basel Conference, which signaled the birth of modern Zionism, a movement of Jewish nationalism that would eventually culminate in the creation of Israel in 1948.

The two monumental events of the twentieth century in Jewish life were not only the reemergence of a Jewish state but the horrifying tragedy and agony of the Holocaust, the systematic attempt by Nazi Germany through genocide to annihilate the Jews of Europe from 1933 to 1945. Here in America, perhaps no one more than Rabbi Stephen Wise demanded a decisive response from Washington to this terrifying calamity. Others, to be sure, joined him in his protests, but to little avail.

More than six million Jews and an additional five million non-Jews perished in the death camps and crematoria. One out of every three Jews in the world was lost in this inferno, but those who survived have prospered and flourished mostly in America and Israel. They, their children, and their grandchildren all attest to a promising new chapter in Jewish history. The past continues to inspire the future.

*Christianity.*    Jesus once asked his disciples, "'Who do you say that I am?'" (Matt. 16:15). That question has driven most of Christian theology for two millennia, for Jesus is undeniably the most important person in Christianity. The history of Christian theology, in fact, consists chiefly of efforts to interpret who Jesus is and how he reconciles humanity to God. The apostle Paul offered some of the earliest written efforts to answer this question in letters he sent to churches throughout the Near East and in Rome. Paul had converted to Christianity after a dramatic encounter with the resurrected Christ during a journey from Jerusalem to Damascus. Paul's most important contribution to the development of the Christian faith was his steadfast insistence that Jesus Christ had come to offer salvation to all of humanity, Jews and Gentiles alike.

During the period of persecution, many Christians looked to the martyrs as heroes of the faith whose example of steadfast trust in God could inspire others to hold fast to their faith during times of hardship. When the period of persecution ended with the conversion of the emperor Constantine, many began to look to the ascetics in the same way. The ascetics were men and women who devoted themselves to lives of prayer and contemplation. Some of them lived solitary lives, and others lived in communities. Asceticism eventually developed institutional form, and communal, monastic life became the norm. Anthony of Egypt and Macrina were two important fourth-century ascetics. Anthony chose a solitary life in the desert outside of Alexandria, Egypt, but he became famous for his changeless faith, and people sought him out for spiritual guidance. Macrina was the sister of two prominent theologians, Basil the Great and Gregory of Nyssa. She never married and instead established an ascetic community within her parents' household. The community attracted women from both the highest social classes as well as those widowed and orphaned by famine. The example of ascetics like Anthony and Macrina inspired generations of Christians.

Next to the apostle Paul, Augustine is probably the most influential theologian for Western Christians. In response to the Donatists, who believed that only the morally pure may serve as priests, Augustine taught that God's grace is extended to sinful humanity through the church even though its ministers are also sinful. In response to Pelagius, who believed that God offers redemption to those who cease to sin through a strenuous exertion of their free will, Augustine taught that human beings cannot free themselves from sin apart from the grace of God. He articulated a theology of culture that encouraged Christians not to shelter themselves from "worldly learning," but to seek out the best of secular learning and to appropriate it for their faith.

By the late eighth century, Europe had been utterly fragmented under the feudalism that grew up in the absence of the centralized authority of the Roman Empire; its population had been decimated by the plague; literacy rates, even among the clergy, were very low; and there was no centralized legal or monetary system. Charlemagne (747–814) forged a "Holy Roman Empire" that temporarily brought some measure of unity to Europe's civil authority. Charlemagne established parish schools to increase literacy and regularized legal codes and monetary units across much of Europe. A generation later, these reforms led to a renaissance in education, law, and theology. The fact that Charlemagne had been crowned emperor by the pope, however, led to centuries of dispute in the West about the degree to which the church should exercise power over civil authorities.

Thomas Aquinas, a thirteenth-century theologian, wrote a summary of theology that offered a new model for how faith and reason are related. He argued that God conveys truth both through revelation (the Bible) and through reason. These two forms of knowledge complement and complete one another. By observing nature we can learn many truths about such things as medicine and ethics, but we can also learn truths about God, such as that God exists and is good. These truths are repeated in the Bible, which adds to them what we must know for salvation. These truths about salvation—such as that Jesus Christ is the Son of God—are not available through reason but are also not contradicted by it. The Roman Catholic Church has embraced the theology of Thomas Aquinas as a faithful articulation of its beliefs.

Martin Luther, along with many other sixteenth-century Protestant Reformers, significantly influenced the development of Christianity. As a young monk he had often been frustrated by his inability to cease sinning. After an extended study of the book of Romans, he came to the conclusion that salvation cannot be earned in any way; it comes as the free gift of God's grace to undeserving humanity. Good works do not merit salvation; instead, good works flow out of human gratitude for the unmerited grace of God. He also taught that Christians persist in their sinfulness—they are, as he put it, simultaneously sinful and justified (or redeemed)—and are never perfected in this lifetime.

John Wesley was an eighteenth-century Protestant in England who became convinced that a faithful life requires more than intellectual assent to Christian beliefs. A faithful life also requires heartfelt love of God and neighbor. He sought to reform the Church of England through the use of small groups devoted to Bible study and prayer. Wesley's movement became known as "Methodism."

Dorothy Day, an early twentieth-century Roman Catholic activist, was the moving force behind the Catholic Worker Movement and founding editor of *The Catholic Worker,* a newspaper that advocated Catholic social teachings. In the midst of the Great Depression, she advocated for workers' rights and a fair living wage. Day opened Catholic Worker Houses that offered shelter and hospitality to the dispossessed. She advocated for women's suffrage and civil rights for African Americans. Day was a pacifist who believed that a just society could ultimately only be achieved through nonviolent means.

Karl Barth, a twentieth-century Swiss theologian, became one of the founders of neoorthodoxy, a response to the theological liberalism of the nineteenth century. In contrast to a theology that emphasized the power of human reason and God's presence in creation, Barth argued that human reason cannot reveal God, but that humanity may only come to know God through a radical act of divine grace. He insisted on God's transcendence, on the "infinite, qualitative difference" between God and creation. Barth wrote in the context of Nazi Germany and became the primary author of The Barmen Declaration, that called the German church to repent of its support for Hitler's regime.

The twentieth century saw a paradigm shift in Christian theology as feminist theologians offered fundamental critiques and reconstructions of the tradition. Rosemary Radford Reuther, for instance, has written extensively on central Christian symbols, analyzing how they have been used to oppress women and how they might be reconstructed in liberating ways. She has offered fresh interpretations of the doctrines of God, Christ, and creation, and has highlighted the connections between the ecological movement and women's liberation.

Martin Luther King Jr. brought deep Christian commitments and theological sophistication to his work in the American civil rights movement. Biblical language and images filled his speeches and sermons, motivating African Americans to rally for their rights and moving the hearts of many white Americans to stand with them. He brought the traditions and cadences of preaching in the black church into his public ministry, calling Americans to organize for justice and to repent of the sin of racism.

*Islam.*    No individual has had more influence on Islam than the Prophet Muhammad. He is considered to be the perfect Muslim, who fully submitted himself to the divine will and put into practice the message of the revelation he was privileged to receive. He is therefore held up as a model of faith on whose example all subsequent Muslims should base their lives. Once Muhammad died, the prophetic model was no longer a living presence among them, and his passing led to the development of an important body of prophetic traditions.

Non-Muslims often assume that the Qur'an serves as a useful record of Muhammad's life that Muslims can consult, but that is not the case. The Qur'an is not about Muhammad at all, and, in fact, his name is found only four times in the text, which contains more than six thousand verses. Instead, Muslims have had to rely on reports of what Muhammad said and did in order to gain detailed information about the Prophet's life. These reports, called hadith, began to circulate soon after Muhammad's death and were eventually gathered together into collections that covered a wide range of topics, including everything from how to pray properly to the most intimate matters of personal hygiene. The hadith have been very influential in Islamic law and personal piety, and they give us a good sense of the central role Muhammad has played in the life of his community.

The most important sources for the hadith were those people who knew the Prophet personally and were therefore in the best position to be familiar with the private details of his life. In fact, the reliability of a given report is based on the identities and reputations of the individuals in the chain of transmission that is an essential part of every hadith. Several groups have been singled out for special recognition in this regard, particularly the "companions of the Prophet" because they knew him well and associated with him on a regular basis. Similarly, Muhammad's wives, especially Khadijah and Aisha, were able to provide a great deal of information about his home life, and therefore many hadith are traced through them. His wives are so highly regarded within the community that they are often given the title "mothers of the faithful."

Among the other individuals who have played a key role in the development of Islam are the various caliphs and other political leaders who have held positions of authority. Within this group, the "four rightly guided caliphs," who governed immediately after Muhammad, were particularly influential in guiding and shaping the early expansion of the faith: Abu Bakr (ruled 632–34), Umar (634–44), Uthman (644–56), and Ali (656–61). Another set of four individuals who had a tremendous impact on theology and social interaction were the founders of the Islamic legal schools: Abu Hanifah (d. 767), Malik ibn Anas (d. 795), Muhammad ibn Idris al-Shafi'i (d. 819), and Ahmad ibn Hanbal (d. 855). Each of them helped to organize and formalize a legal system that continues to play an influential role in Muslim life into the present day.

Several medieval figures were very prominent theologians and intellectuals whose influence sometimes extended beyond the Islamic world. Ibn Sina (980–1037), known as Avicenna in the West, was a brilliant philosopher and physician whose medical textbook was a standard reference work in Europe for centuries. Abu Hamid al-Ghazali (1058–1111) was one of the great minds of the medieval world who made significant contributions in the fields of law, theology, philosophy, and mysticism. Ibn Rushd (1126–98), or Averroes, was a Spanish Muslim who wrote extensive commentaries on Aristotle, and it was through Latin translations of his work that Greek philosophy was reintroduced to the West after a long period of absence.

In the modern period several thinkers have been very influential in determining the role of Islam in the world. Muhammad Iqbal (1877–1938) was an Indian philosopher who was instrumental in the creation of Pakistan. He thought it was vitally important that the strong intellectual tradition within Islam be recovered so that Muslims would be able to address the many issues they need to confront in a world dominated by Western, non-Muslim powers. Another reformer was the Egyptian Muhammad Abduh (1849–1905), who was one of the early pioneers of Islamic nationalism and modernism. In particular he called for a return to a more pristine form of Islam that would be able to respond to some of the social and cultural problems of his time. He was especially interested in issues related to education and improving the place of women in society. A final figure whose influence has been felt in more recent years is Sayyid Qutb (1906–66), an Egyptian who was an outspoken critic of the West and Muslim countries that became too closely allied with the West. He was eventually executed for his views, but he is considered to be the main ideologue and inspiration behind present-day extremist groups like al-Qaeda.

## 3. What places are important for the religion?

*Judaism.*    In Jewish eyes, the Bible emphasizes time much more than space. It sees the world in the dimension of time. It values generations and events much more than countries or things. It assigns higher priority to history than to geography. Appreciating the Bible requires an awareness that time is at least as important to the meaning of life as is space. Time contains a significance and sovereignty of its own.

Curiously enough, in biblical Hebrew there is no equivalent for the word *thing*. In later Hebrew the word *davar* came to denote "thing," because there was no better choice for the purpose, but in the Bible its meaning most often refers to message, report, tidings, advice, request, promise, decision, sentence, theme, story, saying, utterance, business, occupation, act, good deed, or a host of countless other meanings, but never does it mean "thing." The Bible seems to imply that reality is not a matter of "thing-ness."

All holidays and festivals in Judaism celebrate special times, not places or things. Rosh Hashanah is a reminder of creation and the beginning of time, and Yom Kippur is a time for repentance. Even though the major festivals originally were all harvest celebrations, they all came to commemorate historical events in time—Passover, the exodus from Egypt; Shavuot, the revelation at Sinai; and Sukkot, the wandering of Israel in the wilderness. For Judaism these unique events in time were spiritually far more important than the repetitive cycles in nature, however necessary they were to sustain physical life in the world.

Judaism, therefore, as Abraham Joshua Heschel once noted, "is a religion of time aiming at the sanctification of time." No two moments are ever the same. Every passing hour is uniquely precious, special, and memorable.

To be sure, the practice of this reverence for special times required physical places. In earliest times it was probably the Temple at Jerusalem that served that purpose. Even there, however, the place was important only because of the occasions it hosted, especially the plea of the High Priest in the Holy of Holies, the innermost sanctuary, on the Day of Atonement. The sages taught, however, that what mattered most was not even the observance of Yom Kippur, but the day itself, the actual time, which together with human repentance atones for all transgressions.

Today in Israel the most sacred place is probably the Western Wall in Jerusalem, the only remaining portion of the ancient wall that surrounded the outermost courtyard of the Temple. Even here, however, what renders this space most holy is not its physical structure but the faith it symbolizes. It is essentially a repository of precious memories of all the time that has transpired from antiquity to the present day.

No synagogue is sacred because of its physical space. Strictly speaking, there is no such notion in Judaism as "God's house." The location does not matter. Any space can be holy. All that is required for any place to become a synagogue is the presence of a minyan, the minimal numerical requirement for a worship service (ten men in Orthodoxy or men and/or women in Reform and often in Conservative Judaism).

Rabbinic texts stipulate that a synagogue should be clean and beautiful, but that condition is more a preference than a necessity. A synagogue may be little more than a bare room, and no less holy because of its starkness or austerity. This flexibility follows from the Jewish teaching that if God is present everywhere, people may worship God in any place, wherever they may be.

The synagogue, however, serves not just as a place of worship. It is also a "house of study," a school for learning and teaching Judaism for both children and adults alike. In addition, it functions as a "house of the people," a setting where Jews may gather together and strengthen each other in matters of Jewish observance and cultural activities. In short, what sanctifies any space as a synagogue is a matter of what happens there, not where or what it is.

In similar fashion, Judaism attaches special sanctity to the Jewish home. Again, however, what makes that place so special is not the physical space but the values and ideals it embodies and signifies.

In Heschel's words, to understand the meaning of holiness in Judaism, "the sanctity of time came first, the sanctity of man came second, and the sanctity of space last" (*The Sabbath,* 10).

*Christianity.*   Christians acknowledge one God as creator of all that is and believe, therefore, that all things point toward their creator. The world, as John Calvin put it, "is the theatre of God's glory." For this reason any place may become the arena for God's self-revelation, and, in a sense, all places are sacred. Nevertheless, Christians recognize certain places where God has become known in special ways, and these places take on special significance for Christians.

The most important of these places is the space designated for the worship gathering of the community. Often Christians set aside a space, a sanctuary, which is used exclusively for worship. In other instances, the space may be used for other purposes when the congregation is not at worship. In the early church, and in many places throughout the world today, Christians gathered in members' homes for worship. In all cases, the designated space is honored as the space where Christians gather to worship with the expectation that God will meet them in that place and become known to them as the Scriptures are read and as the bread and cup of communion are shared.

Certain cities where central events in the history of the faith have taken place also hold special significance for Christians. Cities and towns where important events in Jesus' life happened—such as Bethlehem where he was born, Nazareth where he was reared, and Jerusalem where he concluded his earthly ministry—have become pilgrimage sites. Constantinople, now Istanbul, houses the ecumenical patriarch for the Eastern Orthodox churches. Rome, the seat of papal authority, is of special importance to Roman Catholics. Protestants look to Wittenburg, a city in Germany, where Martin Luther sparked the Protestant Reformation when he posted his famous "ninety-five theses" on the church door, inviting debate about the nature and extent of papal authority.

*Islam.* The three most holy places in Islam are Mecca, Medina, and Jerusalem. As Muhammad's hometown and the location where the Qur'an was first sent down to him, Mecca is the birthplace of the faith. Muslims are constantly made aware of its importance because they must turn toward Mecca during the five required prayer times each day.

The focal point of the city is the Sacred Mosque, which Muslims consider to be the holiest place on the face of the earth. In the center of the mosque is the Kaaba, the shrine that existed during Muhammad's lifetime and that predates Islam by centuries. According to the Qur'an (2:122–133), the Kaaba was built by Abraham and his son Ishmael as a place of worship dedicated to the one true God. Over time it was converted into a place where polytheism was practiced, and it was restored to its original purpose only with the coming of Muhammad and the rise of Islam.

The Kaaba was originally made of rough, uncut stones, but it has been rebuilt and renovated over the centuries. Today it is a cube-shaped structure about forty-five feet high made of dark-grey stones from the surrounding hills; the stones are usually covered by an intricately decorated cloth covering. Despite its sacred nature, any Muslim is allowed to approach and touch the Kaaba. The King of Saudi Arabia holds the title of custodian of the Kaaba and other sacred places in his country.

Mecca is also important because every year millions of Muslims come to the city to participate in the pilgrimage, one of the five pillars of Islam. Over an eleven-day period during the month of pilgrimage they engage in a series of prescribed rituals that take place in the Great Mosque and the area surrounding Mecca.

While in Mecca many pilgrims take the opportunity to make a journey to Medina to visit key sites in the second holiest city in Islam. Muhammad spent the last ten years of his life there, and Muslims can still see his house and the adjacent Mosque of the Prophet with its distinctive green dome. Other places of interest in Medina include the Shrine of the Prophet, containing his tomb, and Quba Mosque, Islam's first mosque, which was built soon after Muhammad's arrival in the city.

Jerusalem's sacred status can be seen in its Arabic name *al-quds*, which means "the holy." It is the location of two of the most important Islamic buildings, the al-Aqsa mosque and the Dome of the Rock. These edifices are located in what is known as the "Noble Sanctuary" (*al-haram al-sharif* in Arabic), which is the area where the Israelite temple built by King Solomon once stood. The al-Aqsa mosque was built in 710 and is the third most holy place in Islam.

The Dome of the Rock, with its bright golden dome and octagonal shape, is one of the most distinctive buildings in the world. It is not a mosque but a shrine built in 690 to commemorate Muhammad's ascent to heaven. The large rock in the center of the building is held by Muslims to be the place from which the Prophet left the earth to begin the heavenly journey during which he met other prophets from the past. Many non-Muslims visit these two buildings every year, but that is not the case with the sites in Mecca and Medina, cities that allow entry only to Muslims.

Most of the holy places in Shia Islam are found in modern-day Iraq, with two of the most important being Najaf and Karbala. Najaf is the location of the tomb of Ali, the son-in-law of Muhammad and the first Shia leader. It receives thousands of visitors every year, and only Mecca and Medina are more popular pilgrimage destinations in the Islamic world. Najaf, along with Qom in Iran, is also an important center of learning that is the home to a prominent Shia theological school. Karbala's importance for Shia Muslims has already been noted. As the place where Ali's son Husayn was martyred by Sunni forces, it, too, welcomes many pilgrims every year, particularly on the anniversary of that tragic event, when thousands of believers come to the mosque that contains his tomb.

# Chapter Three

# Sacred Texts and Other Writings

## 1. What is the religion's sacred text?

*Judaism.* The basic sacred text of Judaism is not the Old Testament. The proper word is simply the Bible, or the Hebrew Bible. The term "Old Testament" is appropriate only for those who believe that the Bible includes a "New Testament" and choose such a distinction to contrast the two major divisions of their sacred text. Since Judaism does not include a "New Testament," there is nothing "old" about its only Testament. That is why it is fitting to call it simply the Bible. That is the meaning of the term as it will be applied to this explanation of sacred Jewish texts.

The first section of the Hebrew Bible is the five books from Genesis through Deuteronomy whose authorship is attributed to Moses and called by the Hebrew name Torah. Those five books are also known in Hebrew as the *Chumash* ("the Five") and in Greek as the Pentateuch (stemming from Greek and late Latin origins, referring to the first "five scrolls" or books of the Bible).

The second section of the Bible is designated as Nevi'im, which is the Hebrew term for "Prophets." This section includes all the literature attributed to those gifted individuals who were considered recipients of privileged insights into the nature of God and God's purpose. In addition, it includes the books of Joshua, Judges, Samuel, and Kings.

All the remaining books of the Bible constitute the third section, which is understandably known as simply Kethuvim, "The Writings." This portion of the Bible contains some of the finest literature ever written, such as the book of Psalms, Proverbs, Job, Song of Songs, and Chronicles.

All three sections of the Bible comprise a total of thirty-nine books and are known collectively as *Tanakh*, from an acronym derived from a combination of the first letters of each section in their Hebrew terminology (Torah, Nevi'im, and Kethuvim). The actual acronym, *TaNaK*, is the Hebrew word for Bible.

In its most limited sense, the term *Torah* stands for the Five Books of Moses: Genesis, Exodus, Leviticus, Numbers, and Deuteronomy. This section includes the story of creation and the garden of Eden; the contributions of the patriarchs Abraham, Isaac, and Jacob and their families; the enslavement of Israel in Egypt; and the Israelites' liberation from bondage under the leadership of Moses, the most favored of all the prophets. Moses brings Israel to the wilderness of Sinai for the revelation of the Ten Commandments and the entire body of teaching they are expected to follow in their observance of the covenant.

The Torah contains numerous passages that remain forever central to Judaism, such as "You shall love your neighbor as yourself" (Lev. 19:18), and the words of the priestly benediction:

> The LORD bless you and keep you;
> the LORD make his face to shine upon you,
>     and be gracious to you;
> the LORD lift up his countenance upon you,
>     and give you peace.
>                               (Num. 6:24–26)

The eternal Jewish affirmation of faith is also derived from the Torah with the injunction known as the Shema:

> Hear, O Israel, the LORD our God is one Lord; and you shall love the LORD your God with all your heart, with all your soul, and with all your might. And these words which I command you this day shall be upon your heart; you shall teach them diligently to your children, and shall speak of them when you sit in your house, and when you walk by the way, when you lie down, and when you rise up. And you shall bind them as a sign upon your hand, and they shall be as frontlets between your eyes. And you shall write them on the doorposts of your house and on your gates. (Deut. 6:4–9)

This crucial passage from Deuteronomy is taught to a Jewish child almost from the time he/she begins to speak. It is part of every Jewish worship service. Since worship is a daily religious exercise among observant Jews, it is recited every day. Judaism teaches that it should also be the last words on the lips of every Jew who anticipates imminent death. Millions of martyrs ended their lives proclaiming the message of the Shema.

*Christianity.* The sacred text of Christianity, the Bible, is a collection of many different books and letters that include many types of literature. The books that are accepted as Scripture are often referred to as the "canon."

Although there is widespread agreement among Christian churches about what writings are canonical, there are some points of disagreement. We can identify three bodies of work that comprise the Christian canon: the Old Testament, the New Testament, and the deuterocanonical books. These latter are the subject of some dispute.

Christians share with Jews the thirty-nine books of the Tanakh as holy Scripture, though they organize them differently and refer to them as the "Old Testament." The Old Testament consists of the five books of the Law, twelve books of history, five books of poetry and wisdom literature, and seventeen books of prophecy. The Old Testament provides a sweeping account of human history. It begins with a theological interpretation of creation that affirms one God to be the creator of all. It continues with an account of how the tribes of Israel, freed by God from bondage in Egypt, came into the land of Canaan and were ruled by judges. It is impossible to determine when these earliest accounts were written, but around the time the monarchy was established, compilers began to collect both written and oral traditions and to organize them into a coherent narrative. Sometime early in the tenth century BCE, the tribes were united under a single monarch, but by 922 civil war had left them divided into two nations—Israel and Judah. In 722, Israel was defeated by Assyria and its people exiled. Between 586 and 539, Judah was defeated by the Babylonian Empire, and its people exiled. Unlike Israel, Judah eventually returned from exile so that the people were able to maintain their distinctive identity. The Old Testament does not attempt to provide a neutral history of these events. Instead, it offers an interpretation of them in light of God's call to the people to live in covenant faithfulness.

In addition to the thirty-nine books of the Old Testament, all Christian churches accept the twenty-seven books and letters of the New Testament as Scripture. These include four Gospel accounts of the life of Christ, one historical account of the early church, thirteen letters written by or attributed to the apostle Paul, eight general letters, and the Revelation of John, an apocalyptic book. The writings of the New Testament were composed within a century of Christ's death, although it took much longer for the church to identify which works in circulation during this period were canonical. The Gospels—Matthew, Mark, Luke, and John—tell the story of the teaching and ministry of Jesus and of his death and resurrection. The book of Acts narrates the establishment and growth of the church after Christ's ascension. It describes some of the early challenges and controversies the church faced. The letters of Paul provide a window into the life of local congregations when the church was in its infancy. He addresses questions about whether Gentiles must become Jewish to be accepted as Christian, how the Lord's Supper ought to be administered, and how soon Christians might expect Jesus to return to establish the kingdom of God. The general letters and the book of Revelation provide theological lessons, encouragement to Christians who are suffering persecution, instruction about how to treat the poor, and a vision of God's coming reign. All of the writings of the New Testament interpret the meaning of human life and history in light of God's self-revelation in Jesus Christ. They often offer fresh interpretations of the Old Testament in light of the life of Christ, but always remain grounded in the central affirmations of Jewish faith that there is only one God, that God acts in human history (and has acted in the history of Israel in particular), and that God makes a moral claim on human life.

The Roman Catholic and Eastern Orthodox churches also accept certain "deuterocanonical" books that are not part of the traditional Hebrew Bible. Protestants often regard these works as edifying but do not regard them as having the authority of Scripture. These works were largely composed during the period between the end of the Old Testament and the beginning of the New Testament, and some of them, such as the books of the Maccabees, provide an account of that period. These include seven books of history, poetry, and prophecy, as well as additions to the books of Esther and Daniel that are found in the Greek, but not the Hebrew, texts of these books. The Eastern Orthodox canon also includes a few other works, such as Psalm 151, not recognized by either Protestants or Roman Catholics.

*Islam.*   The sacred text of Islam is the Qur'an, an Arabic word that means "recitation." This name is derived from what Muslims believe was the very first message Muhammad received from God, which was in the form of a command: "Recite!" (in Arabic, *iqra'*). The name of the book is also commonly written in English as "Koran," although "Qur'an" is a more accurate transliteration of the Arabic original.

It has already been noted that the Qur'an is considered to be a perfectly preserved record of the revelations Muhammad received from God through the angel Gabriel over the course of the last twenty-two years of his life beginning in 610. The revelations came to the Prophet intermittently throughout those years and, while attempts were made to write down some of them while he was still alive, they were collected together and put in book form only after his death. The Qur'an is the oldest literary text that has come down to us in the Arabic language.

The Qur'an contains 114 chapters of varying lengths with a total of just over six thousand verses, which makes it approximately the same length as the New Testament. Each chapter has a title, which is always some word or name that appears within it. Sometimes these titles refer to an important figure or central theme in the chapter, and at other times it is a very obscure or minor term that appears only once. Examples of chapter titles include the following: "The Cow," "Women," "The Table," "Abraham," "Mary," "The Spider," "Divorce," and "The Disaster." Muslims refer to the chapters by their titles, but there is a tendency among scholars and non-Muslims to identify them by number. Therefore, the chapters listed above can also be identified as 2, 4, 5, 14, 19, 29, 65, and 101. Every chapter but the ninth one begins with the same words: "In the name of God, the merciful one, the compassionate one."

The organizing principle of the chapter ordering appears to be one of length rather than chronology. For example, the command "Recite!" is believed to be the first revelation Muhammad received, but it is the opening word in chapter 96. Similarly, some of the chapters that scholars consider to be the earliest are found toward the end of the book, a clear indication that the Qur'an is not arranged in chronological sequence. But the relative length of chapters does appear to be a factor. After an initial chapter that is fairly brief and serves as an introduction to the book as a whole, the general pattern is one in which the longer chapters come first and the shortest ones are found at the end. The longest chapter in the Qur'an is the second, which runs to 286 verses. At the other end of the spectrum is chapter 108, which contains only three verses.

According to Islamic belief, the original Arabic text of the Qur'an is the only authentic form of the book because this was the language God used to communicate with Muhammad. Any translation into another language is therefore only an interpretation and not truly the Qur'an. For this reason, there are many editions of the text that are bilingual, with the Arabic original on one page and the translated text on the facing page. Because only about 15 percent of the world's Muslims speak Arabic as a first language, the rest have to rely on translations to read their sacred text. All are encouraged to learn the language of the Qur'an, but most lack the opportunity or time to do so. Still, the Arabic form is held in such high regard that it is always read first in mosques throughout the world and then translated into the vernacular.

An aspect of the original text that is easily lost in translation is its poetry. The meter and rhyme that are essential to the Arabic form of the Qur'an cannot be fully duplicated in another language. Even those who do not know Arabic are struck by the beauty and elegance of the text when they listen to it being chanted by someone who is trained in the art of Qur'an recitation. This highlights an important difference between the Qur'an and the Bible. Whereas the Bible is a work that is primarily meant to be read, the Qur'an is one that must be recited and heard to be fully appreciated.

People familiar with the Bible who open up the Qur'an often find it to be a strange and unsettling experience because it does not read like their own text. The Qur'an does not tell a story or follow a sequential order as much of the Bible does. It is a blend of narratives, teachings, warnings, and guidelines whose arrangement can strike the uninitiated as random or haphazard. In addition, the presence of biblical figures and stories in the Islamic Scripture that are similar yet different from their counterparts in the Bible is something Jews and Christians can find confusing.

## 2. How is the sacred text studied and used?

*Judaism.*    The teachings of the Torah are the most sacred legacy and inspiration of the Jewish people. They are so fundamental that they are recited in public reading every week of every year. The five books are divided into segments or portions, one of which is to be read on every successive Sabbath. A segment of each portion is also read during the weekday morning service on Mondays and Thursdays. Usually, the first words of each portion are chosen as the title, so that every week of the Jewish year can be identified by its Torah portion. In Hebrew this segment is called a *sidrah* or parashah. The *sidrah* thus often provides a symbol for the week in which it occurs.

The Five Books of Moses are written in their original form on a parchment scroll by men called *sofrim* ("scribes"), who have devoted their entire lives to copying the words of Scripture by hand, using special ink and goose quills for their task. A Jewish congregation may possess one or several scrolls, since no object in Jewish life is more precious than a Torah. All the scrolls are placed in the *Aron Kodesh* ("holy ark") in the synagogue and are removed only to be read, revered, or repaired.

Each Torah scroll contains exactly the same content. Each is a full text of Genesis through Deuteronomy. If a congregation is blessed with more than a single scroll, it may use one or more for special occasions and another for the weekly reading cycle on each Sabbath. A congregation with only one scroll must continually roll it from the weekly reading to special readings for various holidays and festivals.

Since the Torah is frequently called the "crown of life," it is often decorated with a silver crown or similar symbol of supreme authority. It is wrapped in a festive mantle and may also be embellished with a silver breastplate, the symbol of authority that presumably the high priest wore in the ancient Temple in Jerusalem. Usually the accoutrements also include a *yad* ("hand"), which is a silver ornament in the shape of a human finger and is used as pointer for the leader to follow the reading in the text.

At a designated juncture in certain worship services, the holy ark is opened while the congregation rises. A scroll is removed from the ark and transported to the reading desk on the bimah (from the Hebrew, meaning "platform"). During the delivery of the Torah portion, the congregants are encouraged to follow in Hebrew-English Bibles provided for that purpose.

The *sidrah* is either read or chanted according to an ancient prescribed set of musical modes. The Torah itself contains no vocalization signs, punctuation marks, or musical notations. The leader must know them all through previous training and preparation.

The parashah of the week is usually divided into sections of its own. This permits different members of the congregation to be called to the bimah to offer blessings over the Torah before and after the reading of a particular section. Such an invitation is considered a significant honor and is customarily distributed to the most deserving congregants. Judaism teaches that actually every person is expected to prepare the weekly *sidrah* by examining the text prior to the service and searching every word for its meaning and implications. Tradition dictates that every word of the ancient text is sacred. Any scroll that contains an error is declared deficient or "unkosher" until the error is corrected. A Torah scroll can never be deliberately destroyed or discarded. If it becomes too brittle or too fragile to use, it is buried in the earth just like a deceased person.

The other two major divisions of the TaNaK are not read as frequently in the synagogue as the Torah. The weekly Torah reading, however, does include a selection from one of the two other major divisions of the Hebrew Bible that is referred to as the haftarah (from the Hebrew, meaning "completion"). The haftarah may be a selection from the Kethuvim (Writings) or the Nevi'im (Prophets). Like the Torah portion, it is usually though not always chanted with its own distinctive melody. The haftarah designated for each *sidrah* usually focuses on a theme similar to that in the parashah or includes a reference to a significant individual or event mentioned in the Torah portion. From time to time special occasions will dictate their own particular book of the TaNaK as the haftarah, such as the book of Ruth on Shavuoth, or the book of Jonah on the afternoon of Yom Kippur. Like the Torah portion, the haftarah is also preceded and followed by appropriate blessings.

*Christianity.*    The primary use of the Bible for Christians is as a source for worship. The Psalms, for example, formed the first "hymn book" for Christians. Passages from throughout the Bible are appropriated for liturgical use. A psalm may be read responsively as a call to worship. First John 1:8–9, which says, "If we say that we have no sin, we deceive ourselves, and the truth is not in us. But if we confess our sins, [God] who is faithful and just will forgive us our sins and cleanse us from all unrighteousness," may be used as a call to confession. Other biblical texts may be used to offer an assurance of pardon after the collective prayer of confession. Prayers of illumination, offered before Scripture is read in worship, may also be derived from Scripture. Other passages, such as Matthew 10:8—"Freely you have received, freely give"— may be used as the offering is taken up. Words drawn from the Gospels may be used as an invitation to come to the table for communion, and a passage from 1 Corinthians is always used as the "words of institution" for the Lord's Supper. The Lord's Prayer, which Jesus taught his disciples, and which is recorded in the Gospels, is offered nearly every Sunday in most churches. The words, images, and stories of the Bible provide a rich set of resources from which the language of worship is derived.

A second use, closely related to the first, is homiletical. Because the Bible is understood as an authority for Christian belief and practice, it is read and proclaimed in weekly worship. Sermons usually focus on one or more biblical passages, explaining what they meant in their original context and drawing lessons from that meaning for interpreting the contemporary context. The sermon is understood as an act of worship that frames, interprets, and illumines the meaning of Christian life now in light of the meaning of the Bible. Many churches organize their reading of Scripture around a lectionary, and the sermon will focus on one or more of the lectionary readings for a particular Sunday. The lectionary specifies which texts are to be read each Sunday, usually including a reading from the Old Testament, a psalm, a reading from one of the four Gospels, and a reading from elsewhere in the New Testament. The readings are spread out over a three-year cycle and include portions from every book of the Bible. Christians who regularly attend worship over a three-year period, then, will hear most of the Bible read.

Third, Christians study the Bible in a more academic, critical mode, and the insights gleaned from this mode of study often work their way into sermons. The academic, critical study of the Bible strives to understand the text in its original context. Christian scholars of the Bible strive to uncover the most reliable manuscripts of the Bible in its original languages of Hebrew, Aramaic, and Greek so that they can make good translations. They also compare literary forms used in the Bible to literary forms used by noncanonical sources during the period of its production. This makes it very important to discover when different parts of the Bible were written down, and to understand how ancient the oral traditions behind those written texts might be. Understanding that parts of the book of Isaiah were written before the tribes of Judah were sent into exile by the Babylonians and other parts were written during the period of exile, for example, has shed much light on the meaning of different passages from Isaiah. Some Christians fear that the critical study of the Bible requires treating the Bible as though it were simply a human work and ultimately undermines its authority for Christians. Other Christians, however, find the critical study of the Bible crucial to a proper understanding of it and its authority. Many preachers draw on the critical study of the Bible in their sermon preparation, trusting that a clear understanding of how the Bible was understood in its own time will help them to hear the "word of God" for their own time.

Finally, the Bible is used and studied as a devotional text. As individuals and in small, informal groups, Christians read the Bible as a resource for deepening their spiritual lives and renewing their relationship with God. Many Christians set aside time each day to read the Bible and to pray. Monastic communities have traditionally set aside seven times each day for the "liturgy of the hours," when the Bible is read according to a daily lectionary cycle. During these times, the Psalms take on a central role as they become the prayers offered by the community.

*Islam.*    The majority of Muslims hold a very traditional view of the Qur'an's genesis that is not unlike what many conservative Jews and Christians think about the Bible. They believe that God spoke directly to Muhammad via the angel Gabriel, and that the Prophet was no more than a passive recipient who then communicated the message to his people. The Qur'an is considered to be the verbatim word of God that literally and accurately preserves the content of God's revelations to Muhammad. The words are God's alone, and there was no human involvement or creativity in their origin or arrangement.

This being the prevailing mind-set, critical study of the Qur'an along the lines of what has developed in biblical scholarship does not exist in Islam. The historical-critical study of the Bible that began in the nineteenth century has sought to understand the process by which the text reached its present form. Consequently, it has examined issues related to the possible sources behind the various books and the role that social/cultural contexts have played in influencing the shape and growth of the biblical tradition. One of the results of such study has been the recognition that a wide array of human activity and thought has contributed to the formation of the Bible.

Such a conclusion runs counter to the Muslim understanding of how the Qur'an came to be. The possibility of contextual or human involvement in its origin is repudiated to such a degree that there is a tradition in Islam that says the Prophet Muhammad was illiterate and therefore incapable of either reading or copying anything that could have found its way into God's revelation.

Most Qur'an scholars work within the parameters of these widely held beliefs about the text. There are some Muslims who employ critical methodologies in their work, but they are relatively rare.

Scholarship on the Qur'an has therefore focused more on the text as we have it rather than its history of transmission. It was the first work written in Arabic, and it played a central role in the faith lives of Muslims from the very beginning of the *ummah*, so careful study of the book commenced soon after Muhammad's death. Several aspects of the text have been the subject of scholarly inquiry. One area is Arabic lexicography, the study of the meanings of words. The Arabs were among the first people in history to compile dictionaries, and they often turned to the Qur'an in their efforts to get at the precise meanings of terms. Related to this is the study of Arabic grammar. The early grammarians frequently analyzed the Qur'an to determine how words function together to create meaningful sentences, and many of their discussions about grammatical matters cite specific passages from the sacred text to illustrate their points. Not surprisingly, a third area of study concerns the meaning of the Qur'an, with particular emphasis on the theological messages it seeks to communicate. A vast number of commentaries on the text—often a verse-by-verse consideration of the entire book—have been written throughout history, and many continue to be consulted. It is not uncommon for these theological works also to include discussions of Arabic lexicography and grammar.

Scholarship on the Qur'an has sometimes sought to identify what are referred to as the "occasions of revelation" (in Arabic, *asbab al-nuzul*). Such study is ultimately concerned with context and seeks to determine what was going on within the community or Muhammad's personal life when he received a particular revelation from God. This pursuit attempts to link specific texts to specific contexts in an effort to better understand the circumstances and meaning behind a given passage. Related to this is the division between Meccan and Medinan chapters of the Qur'an. Each chapter is categorized as one or the other depending on whether scholars believe it was revealed before or after Muhammad's journey to Medina. There are ninety Meccan chapters and only twenty-four Medinan ones, but those from Medina tend to be lengthier than those from the earlier period.

Muslims use the Qur'an in ways similar to the ways that Jews and Christians use the Bible. It is recited aloud in communal settings like prayer services and funerals, and it also plays an important role in private devotion. Virtually every Muslim home contains at least one copy of the Qur'an, and it is often prominently displayed where family members and guests can easily see it. It is also common throughout the Muslim world to see a small copy of the text on the dashboards of automobiles or in stores and other places of business. The important role of oral recitation of the Qur'an means that it is frequently present in that form as well. Televised performances of Qur'an reading are a regular part of programming, particularly during religious feasts, and some radio stations play recorded recitation around the clock. These media-based presentations are a constant reminder of the central place Islam's sacred text has in Muslim society.

## 3. What other writings are authoritative for the community?

*Judaism.*   The Tanakh is what Judaism calls the Written Torah. This Written Torah is that document which, so far as we can determine, was initially proclaimed to the people of Israel in relatively complete form by Ezra the Scribe in 444 BCE. The account of that presentation can be found in Nehemiah 9 and 10.

In addition to the Written Torah, a verbal tradition that complemented, clarified, and expanded the Written Torah achieved prominence sometime during the Second Commonwealth. The tradition was known as the Oral Law, in contrast to the Written Law of the Torah.

This Oral Law was a compilation of teachings whose origins probably derived from the dawn of Jewish history and which had been expounded and expanded by each succeeding generation. Traditional Judaism teaches that the contributions of all these generations were revealed to Moses at Mt. Sinai together with the Written Law; therefore they are invested with the same supreme authority as the Torah itself. Again, in the traditional view, the Written Law and Oral Law are inseparable, because both encompass the totality of divine teaching that contains all knowledge for all time to come.

A more historical view of the Oral Law attributes its origins to the limitations of the Written Law in the Torah. This view does not deny the antiquity of these oral teachings by successive generations but contends that they were basically an attempt, through interpretation and amplification, to adapt the Torah to changing times and circumstances. As an agrarian society acquired a more urban character, as a diversity of trades and crafts developed, as the world expanded geographically, it became increasingly urgent to deepen and broaden the application of the Written Law to ensure its relevance and vitality. That was the function of the Oral Law.

In the second century, Rabbi Judah the Prince recognized that the rapidly increasing body of tradition could no longer be preserved and perpetuated orally, even in times of relative peace and tranquility. It was difficult to find scholars who could absorb the enormous quantity of information that had accumulated for several centuries. Rabbi Judah therefore decided to edit in written form the oral traditions of the past.

The Oral Torah was organized into six sections or "orders." This first codification of Jewish teaching following the Written Torah, done in the second century, was called the Mishnah ("Repetition"). Its legal decisions were based on, though not limited to, the Written Law and developed out of intensive discussions and debates among leading scholars. All opinions about the interpretation of Scripture, however, were subject to the test of certain rules or "hermeneutic" explanatory principles that had been formulated by the rabbinic sage Hillel.

The regulations that governed the daily routines of Jewish life and determined the pattern of conduct for all occasions in all places were cataloged under a general rubric called halakah, which is perhaps best translated as "the way" of acceptable Jewish conduct. In addition to halakah, the system also included a body of instruction that explained, expanded, and often embellished the law under consideration by clarifying its principal or larger significance. Such material often followed the pattern of teaching by maxim, legend, or parable, or by a homiletical treatment of the text. This segment of the literature was known as haggadah, which means literally "the telling" of the story, or in modern terminology, preaching.

The haggadah may be found not only as an integral part of the Mishnah but also as a separate literary enterprise attached to the text of Scripture itself and arranged as a self-contained commentary. In this independent form, the material is classified as midrash, which means "the search," with reference to new or hidden meanings in the Written Law.

Halakah and haggadah interact closely and are often exceedingly difficult to separate. One reinforces the other and complements the other. Halakah addresses the question of what a Jew should do, while haggadah explains why he or she should do it.

After the codification of the Mishnah, the same process that had necessitated an expansion of the Written Law now also required an expansion of the Mishnah. Beginning with the rabbinic sages Rav and Shmuel in the third century, the leading scholars examined closely the text of the Mishnah they had inherited and eventually developed a formidable collection of their own interpretations and modifications based on their careful review and scrutiny of the Mishnaic text. The lengthy discussions and decisions they rendered were also committed to writing and were called collectively the Gemara, signifying the "completion" of the Mishnah. The Gemara could always be distinguished linguistically as well as conceptually from the Mishnah by reference to the titles assigned to the teachers of each source. The teachers of the Mishnah were known as the *tannaim* ("teachers"). Those responsible for the Gemara were known to posterity as the *amoraim* ("interpreters").

The fusion of the Mishnah with the Gemara, the combined teachings of the *tannaim* and the *amoraim*, produced the voluminous, supreme classical, post-biblical work of Jewish antiquity, the Talmud. The Talmud is an exceedingly difficult library of books on virtually every conceivable subject of human concern. To be fully understood, it cannot be read casually; it must be studied carefully and thoroughly. Even the serious student would find it almost unintelligible without the contribution of brilliant medieval commentators, the most famous of whom was Rabbi Solomon ben Isaac, better known as Rashi. Rashi and others, especially Maimonides and Nachmanides, wrote running commentaries to almost every sentence and word of the text. Their explanations were placed along the margins of every page of the Talmud.

The text of the Talmud reflects consistently a firm belief in the absolute truth of the Torah, the Written Law. For the rabbinic mind, the truths of the Torah were perfect and immutable. If any statement in the Torah seemed superfluous, contradictory, or obsolete, the problem derived not from the text but from the inadequate understanding of the reader. Indeed, apparent difficulties in the text were often cited as clues or hints to exceptionally profound and mysterious meanings.

If one interpretation did not meet the requirements of the Torah, the only recourse was to change the interpretation, not the Torah. This supreme trust in the process of interpretation may seem contrived to the modern mind, but it was essentially an effort to maintain the continuity of Judaism without tarnishing the integrity of the Torah.

*Christianity.*    In addition to Scripture, Christians accord a level of authority to certain creeds, confessions, and theological writings. After Christianity was legalized under Constantine, a number of theological differences emerged among Christians. There were different ways of interpreting the Bible, different understandings of the person and work of Christ, and divergent views about the nature of human sinfulness. To adjudicate the most serious disagreements, the church established the practice of gathering in ecumenical councils. All of the bishops of the church would meet to discuss and decide matters crucial to the faith. Seven such ecumenical councils were held before the "Great Schism." The first four of these are held in highest esteem by nearly all Christians.

The first ecumenical council was held in 325 at Nicea, where the central question concerned whether or not Christ was truly divine. Everyone acknowledged that Jesus is the Son of God, but there was disagreement about whether the Son and Father were equal in divinity. The council affirmed that Jesus Christ shares full humanity with us and full divinity with the Father. In 381 the church gathered again for the first council of Constantinople. A theologian named Apollinaris had proposed that Christ had a human body but the mind of God. But the council affirmed that Jesus shared our full humanity, including a human mind. The results of these two councils can be found summarized in the Nicene Creed that many churches still use today. This creed holds great authority for almost all Christians and is understood as a faithful guide in interpreting scripture concerning the person and work of Christ. The five other ecumenical councils continued the work of these first two, focusing primarily on questions about the incarnation and the Trinity. They also resolved disputes regarding the use of images in worship and the nature of human sin, affirming that it is appropriate to make images of Christ and that human nature has been so corrupted by sin that no one may achieve salvation apart from the grace of God.

In addition to the seven ecumenical councils and the creeds they produced, there are certain tradition-specific confessions that hold authority for Christians. Confessions are documents that summarize the doctrines considered essential for a particular faith community; they often emphasize certain themes that are distinctive to that community. Among the Presbyterian descendents of English Calvinism, for instance, the Westminster Confession holds a place of special authority. It is understood to be secondary in authority to Scripture but to provide guidance for the proper interpretation of Scripture. This confession begins with an affirmation of the sovereignty of God and includes a treatment of the Ten Commandments. The sovereignty of God and a positive appraisal of the law are two important themes in Calvinism. This confession has also been rendered in the form of two catechisms, a longer and a shorter one. A catechism is a series of questions and answers that are designed to be used as an educational tool for children. Many denominations, including Lutherans and Roman Catholics, rely on confessions and catechisms to summarize their traditions and educate their children.

Occasionally churches produce new confessions, usually in response to some crisis or event that causes the church to rethink its identity and to reaffirm its faith. In many cases the need for a confession is prompted by a threat that, if left unchecked, would undermine the very identity and integrity of the church. During the Second World War, when the Christian Church of Germany had endorsed Hitler's anti-Semitism, a group called "the Confessing Church," led by Karl Barth, issued the Barmen Declaration. This confession renounced the blending of Christian faith with national identity, insisting that the German church ceased to be the Christian church insofar as it sanctioned the Nazi regime.

In addition to creeds and confessions, the writings of certain theologians are regarded as bearing authority. Among Eastern Orthodox Christians, the works of Athanasius, John of Damascus, and Gregory Palamas are held in especially high esteem. These theologians offered interpretations of the incarnation, the Trinity, and the nature of human experiences of God that provide Eastern Christians with concepts and vocabulary that have become essential to their self-understanding as Christians. Augustine stands unrivaled in the West in terms of influence. Although many particular points of his theology may be disputed, his fundamental understanding of God and humanity provides the framework for most Western theology. Thomas Aquinas is especially influential for Roman Catholics. The works of Martin Luther and John Calvin are of special significance for Lutherans and Presbyterians, respectively. And the sermons, hymns, and other writings of John and Charles Wesley hold special authority among Methodists.

*Islam.*    Among the other bodies of writing that play an influential role in Islam the most important are those pertaining to the life of the Prophet Muhammad. The hadith, or traditions about the prophet's life, are second only to the Qur'an in terms of the impact they have had on the community. Because he was considered to be the ideal model for all Muslims, stories about Muhammad's life began to circulate among his followers at a very early stage. These hadith, an Arabic word meaning "report" or "account," usually describe something Muhammad said or did that was remembered by someone close to him.

An enormous number of such traditions began to circulate orally in the early centuries of Islam, and as the religion grew, the hadith spread throughout the Muslim world. Eventually some individuals began to gather together the traditions and study them for accuracy and reliability, a process that culminated in the compilation of several collections. The two most respected and frequently cited hadith collections are those by al-Bukhari and Muslim, two men who both died in the year 870. Each of these works contains several thousand hadith covering a wide range of topics. A popular English-Arabic version of al-Bukhari's collection is nine volumes long and is divided into ninety-three sections, each treating a different topic. The following list of some of the section titles gives a good sense of the range of topics covered by the hadith: belief, menstrual periods, prayers, funerals, pilgrimage, debt, agriculture, prophets, food, medicine, tricks, and God's unity.

The typical form of a hadith can be seen in the following one, in which the prophet Muhammad discusses how long he likes to pray.

> Abdullah bin Abi Qatada narrated: My father said, "The Prophet said, 'When I stand for prayer I prefer to prolong it. But when I hear the cries of a child I cut it short because I do not wish to trouble the child's mother.'"

Every hadith has two parts: a chain of transmitters and a body. In this example, the chain runs from Abdullah bin Abi Qatada to his father to the prophet Muhammad. Some chains are longer than this one and others are shorter, but they all end with Muhammad. The body recounts some statement or action of the Prophet. In this case, the body is his comment about prayer.

Even though it is the less interesting part of a hadith, the chain of transmitters is actually the more crucial component. When al-Bukhari and the other compilers went about deciding which traditions were reliable and which were not, they paid careful attention to who transmitted each hadith. They looked at such things as the personal reputation of each transmitter, whether or not individuals who were linked in the chain were contemporaries and could have known each other, and if the last person in the chain would have been in a position to have heard or observed the Prophet. In this way they attempted to verify the credibility of each chain as a way of determining the probable accuracy of the hadith. Each tradition was placed into one of several categories ranging from strong to weak, and this influenced their decisions regarding which traditions made it into their collections.

The hadith are very popular with Muslims because they give them information and insight into the life of the Prophet. But sometimes they have been a controversial part of Islam. Some scholars question the historicity of the traditions because they can be easily fabricated by simply attaching a strong chain to a spurious saying of Muhammad that would advance one's own personal agenda. Some modern reformers have even argued that Muslims should stop appealing to the hadith. Despite these problems, the prophetic traditions continue to exert great influence over Muslims, especially in the area of Islamic law, where they are the second source used to determine legal rulings after the Qur'an.

Another set of writings that has been important, although less authoritative than the hadith, is the biographies of Muhammad. The most well-known account of the Prophet's life is that written by Ibn Hisham, who died around the year 770. His biography provides a detailed, in-depth account of Muhammad's life and career that fills in the gaps that remain if one tries to reconstruct the events based solely on the Qur'an and the hadith. While the work undoubtedly contains much accurate information about Muhammad's life, some of it is more legendary in nature as it highlights the miraculous in a way that puts him on par with the other prophets.

# Chapter Four

# Leadership and Authority

## 1. What are the important leadership roles in the community?

*Judaism.* There is no hierarchy for religious authority in contemporary Judaism. In ancient times, authority was centered in the high priesthood established by biblical law. The priestly class governed the religious life of the community according to biblical law as detailed especially in the book of Leviticus. They controlled and administered the entire sacrificial system, and since animal sacrifice was the predominant form of worship at that time, the priesthood exercised supreme religious authority. That priesthood, however, ceased to exist after the destruction of the Temple in 70 CE, as did the sacrificial cult.

After the fall of the Second Commonwealth in the first century CE, leadership in ancient Israel centered in the institution of the rabbinate. The role and function of the rabbi actually originated long before the Temple was destroyed but achieved preeminent status in the aftermath of that catastrophe.

The title rabbi is derived from the Hebrew noun *rav*, which in biblical Hebrew means "great" but which does not refer to "rabbi" anywhere in the Bible. In its later sense, in Mishnaic Hebrew, however, the word *rav* means "a master" as opposed to a slave (as, for example, "Does a slave rebel against his *rav*?"—Ber. 10a). It was only in the Tannaitic period, in the generation after Hillel, that it was employed as a title for the sages. The passage in the New Testament (Matt. 23:6–7) in which the scribes and Pharisees are criticized because they "love . . . to have people call them rabbi" probably reflects the fact of its recent introduction. The word *rabbi* therefore means literally "my master" and became simply the title accorded to a sage.

The rabbi of the Talmud, however, was completely different from the present-day holder of the title. The Talmudic rabbi was an interpreter and expounder of the Bible and the Oral Law (Talmud), and almost invariably had an occupation from which he derived his livelihood. He never derived his income from his service as a rabbi. It was only in the Middle Ages that, in addition to or instead of his earlier functions, the rabbi became teacher, preacher, and spiritual head of the Jewish congregation or community.

During the Talmudic period (200 BCE–500 CE) communal leadership was vested in a body called the Sanhedrin, which consisted of seventy rabbinic sages who governed as both a legislative and judicial institution, but the Sanhedrin also no longer functioned after the sixth century.

Since the European emancipation of Jews in the eighteenth century, the role of the rabbi has radically changed. In the first place, governments in various countries insisted that Jews follow the civil laws of the state like everyone else, which then made the role of rabbi as judge in civil litigation obsolete. Even matters of ritual and matrimonial law that the Jewish community could still control fell under the jurisdiction of a central *bet din,* a Jewish court of law composed of specialists in this area.

In addition, as Jews became more acculturated into the general life of the larger world, they realized clearly the necessity for rabbis to acquire wider knowledge than they previously possessed. They needed to be grounded not just in Jewish sources but in purely secular branches of learning as well. The incentive in that direction only accelerated when a number of countries required a certain standard of general education as a condition of recognizing rabbis.

Although numerous Orthodox seminaries refused to permit any change in their traditional curricula that consisted entirely of Talmud and the subsequent codes of law, other rabbinic seminaries emerged that provided a comprehensive course of study that blended Jewish sources with a standard university education. The modern rabbi, then, whether Orthodox, Conservative, or Reform, is largely the product of these more progressive centers of learning.

During the Middle Ages, until the emancipation of the nineteenth century, central Jewish authorities arose occasionally in certain European countries. The United Synagogue of Great Britain, for example, still appoints a Chief Rabbi of the country and maintains strict control over matters of conversion, marriage, and divorce.

The Israel Chief Rabbinate is also granted authority by the government in all matters relating to personal status of Jewish residents in that country. Non-Orthodox segments of the Jewish community have achieved limited recognition but still do not share in the power apparatus of the Jewish religious establishment.

*Christianity.*    Earliest Christian communities gathered to share a meal commemorating the life, death, and resurrection of Jesus (the Lord's Supper). They read and interpreted accounts of the life of Christ, letters from apostles, and

Scripture from the Hebrew Bible. They prayed together, took up collections for the poor and for widows, and discussed matters of importance in their community. They also proclaimed their faith in Christ to others and received new members into their community through the sacrament of baptism. Leadership roles within the church emerged in response to these practices, and as the church grew and developed an institutional structure, these leadership roles became increasingly differentiated and specialized. These same basic functions, however, continue to determine the shape of leadership in the Christian church today. Leaders in Christian communities, that is, live as servants whose function is to assist the church in its worship, ministry, and evangelism.

With very rare exceptions, Christian communities ordain certain individuals to lead the community as clergy. Of all of the practices of the church, two kinds of activities, which are understood to be means of grace, are especially entrusted to the clergy. These means of grace are hearing the word read and proclaimed and receiving the sacraments. The clergy are responsible for planning the weekly worship of the church so that the means of grace are regularly made available to the people. In worship, clergy offer prayers on behalf of the congregation, deliver sermons that retell and interpret the sacred stories of the faith, and administer the sacraments of the Lord's Supper and baptism. Clergy also offer pastoral care to members of their congregation and coordinate the other ministries of the church. They usually undertake a specialized program of theological education, requiring both a bachelor's and a master's degree, so that they are prepared to lead the community in these ways.

Another important leadership role in the church emerged in the fourth century after the period of persecution had ended. This was the role of the monk, an individual who remains unmarried and is devoted especially to a life of prayer and contemplation. Monasticism developed into a variety of forms, both solitary and communal, for both men and women (who are sometimes called nuns). Monks usually live according to a "rule," a set of practices that govern the community. Such a rule might determine how often they gather for prayer, how many hours a day are devoted to work or to rest, when mealtimes will be, what responsibilities various members of the community have, and how the tasks of the community are distributed among its members. Monastic orders organized themselves around particular ministries: some are devoted to ministries with the poor; others, to study and education; and yet others, to spreading the faith to new places. Traditionally the office of the monk was separate from the office of ordained clergy, but now the two often go together so that it is not uncommon for male monks also to serve as priests.

Laypeople serve many important leadership roles in the church and may even be ordained or consecrated to offices such as elder or deacon, though these terms are not always used or used in the same way. Usually elders and deacons are laypersons who have been chosen by their congregations to serve on the governing board of the congregation for a set amount of time. The governing board may be known as the "session," "consistory," "vestry," or by some other term. Members of this body typically make decisions about how church property may be used, develop the budget and disburse funds, assist the pastor by visiting sick and elderly members of the congregation and bringing the bread and wine used in the Lord's Supper to those unable to be present for worship, coordinate the educational programs of the congregation, prepare the sanctuary for worship, and assist in worship leadership—among many other things.

Educators, who may or may not be clergy, also play an important leadership role in the Christian church. Because belief and doctrine are so central to Christian faith, Christians have historically placed a high value on educating their children and new converts about what Christians believe and on nurturing faith throughout one's lifetime through continuing education. Many educators are lay Christians who lead children, youth, and adults in weekly "Sunday school" meetings where they read and interpret Scripture together, discuss the relationship between their faith and current events, learn new devotional practices, and so forth. Other educators who work in congregations have sought advanced training and certification to become professional Christian educators. They often serve as resources persons for a congregation, identifying appropriate curricula for various age groups and training Sunday school teachers in their use. Still other educators serve in colleges and universities or in seminaries, where they train future pastoral leaders for the church.

Finally, Christian churches have always sponsored missionaries who bring the gospel to new places. They serve as evangelists but also as ministers to the poor and outcast, as advocates for justice, and as educators. Missionaries may be clergy, monks, or laypeople. They may serve in this vocation for a lifetime or for a set number of years. In recent years, some Christians have undertaken short-term mission projects. Christians with medical training, for instance, may serve for a few weeks in an impoverished or remote area, where there is little access to health care.

*Islam.*    Because he is the standard for Muslims in every time and place, the Prophet Muhammad continues to play a central leadership role within his community centuries after his death. Many Muslims look to his example and intentionally model their own lives on what he said and did as recorded in the hadith collections and other Islamic sources. Muhammad therefore remains the ideal figure within whose shadow all subsequent leaders must function and operate.

In the early period of Islamic history religious authority and political authority were often joined together and associated with one individual. This was considered to be in line with the precedent established by Muhammad, who was both a prophet of God and a statesman during his lifetime. For example, the "Rightly Guided Caliphs"—the four men who ruled the Islamic community after the death of the Prophet (632–661 CE)—were held to be the final authorities in all matters of religion and politics. As Islam spread during their reigns they had a profound impact on shaping both the physical and spiritual dimensions of the emerging empire.

But this situation did not continue for long. For a variety of reasons it soon became clear that it would be better to separate religious authority from political authority, and that is the arrangement that continues to be operative in most of the Islamic world to the present day. Consequently, leadership in Islam is primarily exercised within the spiritual realm in a way that is similar to what is found in Judaism and Christianity.

But there are some key differences among the three faiths in this area. One of the most important is the lack of a clergy or institutional hierarchy in Islam. While there are authority figures in the religion, there is no equivalent to the priesthood or the rabbinate in Islam. Within the context of worship, the most important role is played by the imam, who serves as the prayer leader. Most mosques, especially large ones, have a permanent imam who functions in this capacity on a full-time basis. In smaller mosques it is more common to rotate leaders from among the community so that no one person is identified with the role. The backgrounds and qualifications of imams vary considerably and they function independently of each other. The lack of a hierarchy or level of authority above them—as seen, for example, in the Catholic Church, where the bishops are the superiors of priests—makes this autonomy and independence possible.

Beyond the area of ritual and worship there are other individuals who function as leaders within the community, and some of these will be mentioned below. But when it comes to the daily lives of the vast majority of Muslims, it is the imam, more than anyone else, who is looked to as an authority figure. It should be noted, however, that there is some possibility for confusion over the precise meaning of the term imam because it means one thing to Sunni Muslims and another thing to Shia Muslims.

What has been described above more accurately reflects the practice and understanding of Sunnis, for whom imam is a generic term referring to any prayer leader.

For Shia Muslims, though, the word denotes a particular individual who is the leader of their community par excellence. The Shia believe so strongly that the Prophet Muhammad is the quintessential authority figure for Muslims that they maintain that only a descendant of the Prophet can properly lead them. For this reason they often refer to themselves as "the people of the house" (in Arabic, *ahl al-bayt*), an allusion to Muhammad's genealogical line.

According to Shia belief, after the death of Ali, the fourth of the "Rightly Guided Caliphs" and the son-in-law of the Prophet, leadership was passed on to his two sons and then to their sons, forming an unbroken chain that could trace its roots back to Muhammad. Each of these leaders was called the imam, and he exercised complete authority over the Shia community during his lifetime. The chain came to an abrupt halt in the ninth century CE, when the twelfth imam had to go into hiding out of fear for his life. Shia Muslims believe he is still in hiding somewhere in the world and will return at some future point.

The reason that the twelfth imam was forced to flee was that Shia Muslims have often been oppressed by the majority Sunnis. In order to ensure his survival the imam was taken into hiding by God until he can claim the leadership of the entire Muslim community that is rightfully his. While most Shia believe it was the twelfth imam who went into hiding (and are therefore called "Twelvers"), there are a few sects that maintain it was actually the seventh imam. The entire community believes that in the interim between his departure and return, authority rests in a group of religious leaders among whom are the Ayatollahs, whose title literally means "sign of God."

## 2. How are the roles of leadership and authority exercised?

*Judaism.*    The function of the modern rabbi varies somewhat in various countries, depending on local conditions. Preaching in the vernacular, of course, occupies a place of prime importance out of all proportion to the earlier model of the rabbi, who generally limited his public discourses to two addresses per year, usually on Yom Kippur and on the Sabbath preceding Passover.

The modern rabbi is expected to devote much of his time to pastoral work, establishing a personal bond between himself and his congregants. Those duties include visiting the sick and officiating at bar mitzvah ceremonies, marriages, funerals, and houses of mourning, as the occasions require. The rabbi is expected as well to take part in all social, educational, and philanthropic activities of the synagogue. Above all, he is seen as the spokesman, the ambassador of the Jewish community to the non-Jewish world.

In recent times, however, rabbis not only serve as spiritual leaders of their synagogues; they also find opportunities as directors of Jewish student organizations on college campuses; as executive officers of Jewish defense organizations, such as the Anti-Defamation League or the American Jewish Committee; and as administrative heads of local Jewish federations and welfare funds. Quite a few rabbis now work either as military chaplains in the armed services or as hospital chaplains in various health-care facilities. A number of rabbis even continue their studies beyond ordination to earn advanced degrees that qualify them to teach on college and university faculties across the country.

In the United States there is no central Jewish authority, either religious or communal. Every synagogue is completely autonomous; a congregation affiliated with one branch of Judaism may, whenever it so decides, join another movement. The rabbi of each synagogue is chosen by a vote of its membership and is not assigned to it by any national body.

The American Jewish community does not include any equivalent of a bishop or adjudicatory head. No rabbi possesses the power to determine the status of a colleague or to place him in a pulpit.

Similarly, there are no regional or state authorities. Even the New York Board of Rabbis, with a membership in the hundreds, has no adjudicatory powers. The Board helps develop standards for Jewish religious life and uses its moral influence in civic and synagogue affairs, but it is a purely voluntary body, whose influence stems solely from the goodwill and respect of its supporters.

Each of the three major movements in American Judaism support two national organizations, one of them an association of its member congregations, the other its national rabbinic body. In Orthodox Judaism, the lay leadership is centered in the Union of Orthodox Jewish Congregations; its rabbinic counterpart is the Rabbinical Council of America. The United Synagogue of America serves as the congregational arm of Conservative Judaism, and the Rabbinical Assembly, as its rabbinic body. In Reform Judaism, the Union of Reform Judaism is the national voice for laypeople, and the Central Conference of American Rabbis is its rabbinic arm.

All these organizations are voluntary associations of laypeople and spiritual leaders who have joined together to share experiences, develop standards of principle and action, and engage in collective projects and activities to advance their goals and aspirations.

Whatever discipline American synagogues accept is self-imposed. Their national bodies do not interfere with the internal affairs of a particular synagogue in matters of worship, administration, structure, or the selection of a specific rabbi or staff member. The influence of these parent bodies is purely moral: they may urge standards of ritual and worship, but they cannot compel conformity. Consequently, the three major movements exhibit a wide range of diversity in most matters of religious observance.

The rabbinical associations reserve the right to expel members from their own ranks, but only the theological seminary grants the title of rabbi, and it alone has the power to withdraw a rabbi's ordination. From a practical point of view, such discipline is exercised rarely, if ever, either by the seminary or the professional association.

In terms of leadership and authority, American Jewish religious life possesses several other distinctive features. Religious activities are not, as in other countries, exclusively under synagogue control. The religious life of Jewish college students is served largely by a lay organization called the Hillel Foundation, originally funded by B'nai B'rith. Another lay body, the National Jewish Welfare Board, addresses the spiritual needs of Jewish men and women in the armed services. Though rabbis cooperate with and even serve both these groups, neither is under rabbinic control.

Every American Jew is also completely free to choose whatever branch of Judaism he/she prefers. Unlike British Jewry, whose official national synagogue is Orthodox, or French Jewry, whose official religious authority is liberal Orthodox, the three American groups, Orthodox, Conservative, and Reform, all enjoy equal status. The Synagogue Council of America, a coordinating organization of the three groups, selects officials from all three branches. And the very existence of this range of religious expression precludes any central authority for American Jews.

*Christianity.*    The polity, or form of governance, of a particular church determines how it selects leaders and interprets the nature of their authority. Christian churches organize themselves in a wide variety of ways, but we can identify three basic models of polity: episcopal, congregational, and presbyterian.

The episcopal polity derives its name from the Greek word for bishop, and is so named because churches that use this polity are governed by bishops. The Roman Catholic, Eastern Orthodox, and Anglican/Episcopalian churches all have episcopal polities. Methodist and some Lutheran churches also use a modified episcopal polity. These churches note that the New Testament uses several different terms for church leaders, including the terms "bishop" and "elder," and argue that these terms specify different functions and different kinds of authority. Elders serve as pastors to local congregations, while bishops, who are understood as the successors of the apostles, supervise and direct the elders within their jurisdiction. The jurisdiction of a bishop is called a diocese and is usually a geographic area. Bishops have the power to ordain new priests (elders) to office and to determine which congregations they will serve.

The pattern of hierarchy that distinguishes bishops and local priests extends also to distinguish between clergy and laity. Episcopal polities usually draw a sharp distinction between clergy and laity. Clergy are understood to have a special call from God that differs qualitatively from the call that the laity receive to become, say, physicians, carpenters, or attorneys. This call sets them apart to function as priests who mediate between God and the people, and their ordination leaves what Roman Catholics call an "indelible mark" of character that sets them apart from others.

There is also a hierarchy that distinguishes different kinds of bishops. In the early church, bishops of the major cities emerged as leaders over other bishops. Their jurisdiction, called a synod, encompassed several dioceses. In Eastern Orthodox communions these bishops-of-bishops became known as patriarchs, and eventually the patriarch of Constantinople, who is called the ecumenical patriarch, emerged as the preeminent bishop. In Roman Catholicism these bishops became known as archbishops, and the bishop of Rome— the pope—emerged as preeminent.

Congregational polity constitutes a second way in which authority is organized among Christian churches. Congregationalists focus, as their name implies, on the local congregation as the locus of authority. They may form associations that set guidelines for member congregations, but power fundamentally flows from the local congregation to the association. Baptists, independent/nondenominational congregations, and the United Church of Christ operate with congregational polities. Congregationalists argue that the New Testament teaches that it is the concrete gathering of the community, and not a hierarchical institutional structure, that is the church, the body of Christ. Congregationalists believe that each local community should call its own leaders rather than have them appointed by a bishop. Those leaders, moreover, are under the authority of the local congregation.

Congregational polity also differs from episcopal polity in its understanding of the relationship between clergy and laity. Congregationalists generally do not draw a sharp distinction between the two. They believe that all Christians have a vocation; that is, all Christians are called by God to take up certain tasks for which they have particular gifts. The call to serve as a physician, carpenter, or attorney is not qualitatively different from the call to serve as a pastor. The difference between clergy and laity, then, is simply a difference of function, not a difference of status. Clergy have gifts that enable them to preach and administer the sacraments effectively, and so they are designated by the local congregation to take responsibility for these functions. But clergy are not priests; they do not mediate between God and the people; only Christ does that. Rather, all Christians have equal status before God.

Presbyterian polity offers a third way in which Christian churches organize authority. Presbyterian and Reformed denominations use this polity, which they also see as based on a New Testament model. The term "presbyterian" comes from the Greek term for "elder." Churches using a presbyterian polity note that while the New Testament does use different terms for church leaders, such as bishop and elder, it does not consistently distinguish or establish a hierarchical relationship between these. Instead, the New Testament church seems to have included different kinds of leaders who worked together as colleagues and peers. So, Presbyterian and Reformed churches are governed by elders who work collaboratively to ensure that all of the purposes of the church are pursued with integrity. This collaborative model of authority means that no one person is ever vested with final authority on matters of doctrine or practice. Instead, decisions about belief and practice are always made by groups of elders and are always subject to future review by other groups of elders.

The most basic level at which elders gather to govern the church is at the level of the local congregation. Here elders meet in what is known as the session, consistory, or council. The session will consist of ruling elders who are laypersons elected by the congregation to serve for a set term and will be moderated by a teaching elder who is clergy. Like the congregational polity, presbyterian polity assumes that function, not authority, distinguishes clergy and laity. Clergy are responsible for the means of grace, and lay elders take responsibility for other aspects of church life.

The next level at which elders (both lay and clergy) gather to govern the church is at the presbytery, which consists of all of the local congregations in a certain geographic area. Beyond the presbytery one finds synods that encompass several presbyteries. Finally, elders gather at a General Assembly of the entire denomination. Decision-making authority always flows from the local congregation, through the presbytery and synod, to the General Assembly. But those decisions are subject to review at those more general levels. Likewise, decisions made at the more general level must always be ratified at the local level.

*Islam.*    Most imams have some kind of formal education in Islamic theology, although this is not a requirement for the office. Any good Muslim with an unblemished reputation and a well-developed understanding of the faith is qualified to function in this capacity. Those who have attained a degree in

Islamic theology have normally done so at one of the many centers of learning found throughout the Muslim world.

In a small number of countries, the imams are assigned to mosques by the government. This is commonly done throughout the world when the mosque in question is a prominent one of historical importance. Generally speaking, the lack of an institutional hierarchy means there is no overseeing body that determines which imam serves where. Such decisions are usually made at the local level by the members of the individual mosque.

A major responsibility of the imam is to be the leader during the five prescribed prayer times throughout the day. This entails standing facing the *mihrab*, the niche that indicates the direction toward Mecca, with his back to the congregation. All in attendance face in the same direction behind the imam, and they take their lead from him on when to do the prayers, bows, and protestations that comprise Islamic prayer. The imam's role in leading communal prayer is the primary reason why the office is reserved for men. The various body movements of the prayer cycle would put a woman in a potentially embarrassing physical position in front of the praying men, a situation to be avoided. The distractions that would result from having members of the opposite sex in close proximity to one another is an additional reason often cited for separating the men and women during prayer.

Another important task the imam performs is to give the sermon at the noon prayer gathering on Friday, the holy day of the week in Islam. At a particular point in the service he moves over to the pulpit, a symbol of his authority, and reads a portion of the Qur'an to the congregation. In countries where Arabic is not the native language, the text is first read in Arabic and then translated into the local language. After the reading is concluded, the imam then delivers the sermon, which usually draws upon the Qur'an passage or comments on some aspect of it. As is the case in similar addresses given by worship leaders in Judaism and Christianity, the imam's sermon typically contains a combination of textual analysis, moral instruction, and exhortation on how to apply the reading's message to one's personal life.

In addition to these formal activities, the imam serves in a variety of capacities that mirror very closely those associated with priests, ministers, and rabbis. He is the person to whom members of his mosque turn in matters related to their spiritual well-being. He offers advice and council to those who are experiencing problems in their personal or professional lives. He visits the sick and the dying and attempts to comfort them and their loved ones. He is involved in the religious education of his congregation on both the individual and communal levels. When they have questions regarding what Islam teaches about a particular social issue they turn to him.

There is no ordination service or similar ceremony that officially designates someone an imam and formally recognizes his readiness to function as a leader. Similarly, Islam lacks any sacraments or other rituals that can only be performed by him and therefore set him apart from the rest of Muslims. Any male member of the community can lead prayer, give the sermon, and officiate at a funeral or wedding. Consequently, there is a very strong sense of equality among all Muslims because there is no group or class of individuals whose role in the community gives them a special status or distinguishes them from the rest by virtue of their ability to perform certain functions reserved only for them. Those in a position of authority are no different from the others, and their authority is always exercised for the good of the group as a whole.

As noted above, in Shia Islam various religious leaders play leadership roles in the absence of the hidden imam. These are jurists and theologians who are trained in the religious sciences and therefore qualified to lead the community on behalf of its missing leader. These men play a more prominent role than the imam in Sunni Islam since their authority extends beyond leading prayer and delivering the weekly sermon. Leaders with titles like Hujjat al-Islam ("Proof of Islam") and Ayatollah possess a great deal of authority because they are able to perform important tasks like render legal verdicts and formulate doctrine.

## 3. Who else has authority in the community?

*Judaism.*    Rabbis are not the only individuals who exercise influence in the Jewish community. They share their authority with other Jewish professionals and lay leaders. The most notable of these in the synagogue domain is the cantor. The cantor, or, in Hebrew, the *chazzan,* is a Jewish musician trained in the vocal arts who helps lead the synagogue in chanting and musical prayer.

The idea of a cantor as a paid professional does not exist in classical rabbinic sources but is a development of relatively recent vintage. Judaism permits any person to lead the congregation in public worship, which is why such an individual is called the *shaliach tzibur,* or "emissary of the congregation." In more observant circles, Jewish law requires the *shaliach tzibur* to be a male over the age of thirteen. In non-Orthodox practice, women over the age of twelve are also eligible.

The term *chazzan* may have been borrowed from the Assyrian word *hazanu,* which in the Talmud is used to denote the "overseer" either of a city, a court of justice, the Temple, or the synagogue. It also comes from the word *chazzon* or "visionary." The earliest *chazzanim* (the plural of *chazzan*) were most likely prophets. In regard to a *chazzan*'s duties in the synagogue, the Talmud notes that two thousand years ago, he brought out the scrolls of the Torah, opened them at the appointed readings for the week, and put them away again. With trumpet blasts he announced the beginnings of the Sabbath and holy days from the roof of the synagogue, attended to the lamps of the synagogue, and accompanied pilgrims to the sanctuary of Jerusalem. He would often stand on the wooden bimah (platform) in the middle of the synagogue and sometimes chant aloud from the Torah. A passage in the Jerusalem Talmud (Ber. 9:12d) implies the *chazzan* also led the prayers in the synagogue.

During the Middle Ages, the duties of reading from the Torah and of reciting the prayers were usually included as standard duties of the *chazzan*. He was also recruited to sound the shofar (the ram's horn). He even acted sometimes as secretary to the congregation. He was often assisted, especially on festival days, by a chorus, which later developed in Poland and Germany into a custom wherein a singer stood on each side of the cantor and accompanied him.

In the modern synagogue, the cantor leads the worship service and therefore must be fluent in all aspects of the liturgy. This includes, of course, knowledge of the meaning of the Hebrew words he/she is chanting and complete familiarity with the musical modes for various occasions, as well as the laws and customs of the liturgical calendar.

During the last half-century, cantorial duties have expanded even further to include the teaching of bar/bat mitzvah classes, Hebrew school teaching, adult education programs, leading or working with a choir, and concertizing in his/her own community and beyond.

The role of the cantor as a respected full-time profession became a reality only in recent centuries. A number of European communities, especially Germany and England, considered professionally trained cantors as clergy. After the Enlightenment, when Jews gained full citizenship and civil rights, many secular governments granted cantors the same clergy status as rabbis. The United States, in fact, recognized cantors as the first Jewish clergy, even before any rabbis had arrived in America. Today in this country three major schools exist for the professional training of cantors. Each major movement in Orthodox, Conservative, and Reform supports its own institution for this purpose.

Since there is no ecclesiastical authority in Judaism, leadership is a shared responsibility between clergy and laypeople. Synagogue and communal organizations are governed entirely by lay leaders, almost always as volunteers. Synagogues, for example, are usually founded by laypeople and administered by them, including the recruitment and supervision of professional personnel. The rabbi's authority in religious matters rests only on the presumption of his greater knowledge of Judaism, not on any priestly or ecclesiastical status. The modern synagogue is emphatically a democratic institution in which all major decisions are made by a governing board of directors or by the membership of the congregation itself.

*Christianity.*    There are two important groups who always carry authority in Christian churches even when official doctrine and polity do not acknowledge them: women and the wealthy. Women have been active leaders since the beginning of the Christian faith. Jesus violated social norms by conversing with and teaching women. He included them among his innermost circle of followers. Many of the most important turning points in his career were marked by interaction with women. In the Gospel of John, he is first made known as messiah to the woman at the well. In the Gospel of Mark, he begins his ministry among the Gentiles after a woman argues with him. In all of the Gospel accounts it is women who first attest to the resurrection. Other New Testament writings confirm that women continued to be active in leading the early church. The apostle Paul mentions a number of important women in his letters and even identifies one of them, Junia, as an apostle.

But the status of women in the New Testament is also mixed. In one place women are admonished not to speak during worship, in other places they are forbidden to teach, and in another they are taught to submit to their husbands. Although these texts are difficult to square with the others previously mentioned and with the basic Pauline affirmation that in Christ differences of status such as male and female have been abolished, the ambiguity about the status of women in the New Testament eventually led the church, in conformity with its surrounding Greco-Roman culture, to the conclusion that women are subordinate to men and may not serve as leaders in the church.

Most Christian churches still forbid women to serve as clergy. The Roman Catholic and Eastern Orthodox churches, together with most Baptists and independent/nondenominational churches, teach that women may not hold ordained office. Other Protestant denominations, however, permit and encourage women to serve in all areas of church leadership. African American churches were among the first to affirm the gifts of women for ministry. The Methodists, most Episcopalians and Presbyterians, the United Church of

Christ, most Lutherans, and others followed. Even in denominations and congregations where they are not permitted to hold church office, however, women still carry a great deal of authority. Sometimes that authority is acknowledged—when they serve as Sunday school leaders for children, organize and volunteer in church ministries, and so forth—and at other times it takes the form of behind-the-scenes influence.

The wealthy also carry a great deal of authority in Christian churches even though it violates deeply held Christian convictions to privilege them. In spite of the church's best efforts to uphold the poor and to hold all as equal, Christians have often succumbed to social and cultural pressures that favor the wealthy and give them undue influence on the policies and practices of a community. It is not uncommon to find that those who can afford to make the largest financial contributions to a congregation are also those most likely to be chosen for service as leaders. Their influence is also felt when congregations deliberate on controversial matters because of fear that an unpopular decision may threaten the financial stability of a congregation if wealthy members decide to leave or to withhold funds because of that decision.

*Islam.*    Up to this point, we have concentrated primarily on authority in Islam as it pertains to ritual and worship. But other types of leadership are also found within the Muslim community, with two of the most important being intellectual authority and charismatic authority. Intellectual authorities exert a tremendous amount of control over the lives of Muslims. Scholars who are trained in Islamic theology and related fields are the ones responsible for determining proper belief and appropriate behavior among members of the community. Islam is a religion of orthopraxy, or proper action, so how one lives one's life and puts his or her faith into action has always been an important matter. Law is the discipline that is most concerned with regulating and monitoring human conduct, so it should come as no surprise that jurists and legal scholars have been among the most important authority figures in the faith.

Laws began to be established and codified in the early centuries of Islam, and by the ninth century BCE four main schools of law named after their founders had been established: the Maliki school, the Hanbali school, the Shafi'i school, and the Hanafi school. These continue to be the dominant schools for Sunni Muslims into the present day, but Shia law operates under a different framework. The differences among the four are usually not very significant, but they are distinct enough that it is not uncommon for legal opinions to vary from school to school. A Muslim is free to consult a lawyer affiliated with any of the four schools in order to seek legal advice, which is then used in rendering a verdict or reaching a decision in the specific case.

The decision is usually handed down by a mufti, who is the individual responsible for issuing the formal legal verdict, or fatwa. In many Muslim countries the government appoints one individual who functions as the Grand Mufti, or official head of the legal establishment. Sometimes a leader will act on his own to issue a fatwa that addresses some issue or concern that he considers to be particularly important. Because of the important roles played by muftis, judges, and lawyers in determining and enforcing Islamic law, these individuals possess a great deal of authority within the Muslim community. They exert influence on matters as far-reaching as what Muslims should believe and as personal as the terms of inheritance within a particular family. They are considered to be the intelligentsia within Islamic societies, a status that is reflected in the term used to refer to the body of legal scholars as a whole—the 'ulama', or "learned ones."

Another form of authority is of a more charismatic nature and is primarily associated with Sufism, the mystical branch of Islam that traces its roots back to the earliest days of the faith. Each of the many Sufi groups, often called brotherhoods, is organized around the teachings and practices of its founder. The members of the group commit themselves completely to the lifestyle and philosophy of their founder in a way similar to what occurs among members of Christian religious orders like the Franciscans. A basic premise of Sufism is that the individual must progress through a series of states and stages until finally reaching the goal of self-extinction and an experience of oneness with God. To realize this objective the individual Sufi must come under the authority of a master or sheikh, a member of the group who has successfully passed through the various stages. This spiritual leader, carrying on the tradition and charism of the founder, becomes the supreme authority figure for the student. A well-known proverb says that the relationship between the Sufi and the master must be like that between the corpse and the person who washes it in preparation for burial.

Founders of Sufi orders and other holy men and women often affect the lives of people far beyond their circle of disciples. These individuals are considered to be specially blessed by God, and places associated with them often become pilgrimage destinations for other Muslims, who will sometimes travel great distances to reap spiritual benefits from praying at their monasteries or tombs. Stories and texts circulate about the lives of these holy people that often include examples of their teachings and descriptions of miracles they performed. Such accounts contribute to their status as authoritative figures whose lives should be emulated by others, but this area of Islamic spirituality is not without its controversies. Critics consider it to be a kind of veneration of saints that violates the spirit of Islam, and it is outlawed in a few Islamic countries. But the fact that these charismatic figures and the practices associated with them continue to thrive in many parts of the world demonstrates that this is an important part of Muslim popular religiosity.

Chapter Five

# Beliefs

## 1. How is the human condition understood in the religion?

*Judaism.* Judaism teaches that a person is neither inherently good nor inherently evil. Every individual is born with two conflicting inclinations. One is called the *yetzer hatov*, the passive or receptive impulse; the other is called the *yetzer hara*, the active or aggressive impulse. The *yetzer hatov* is the innate drive for all creative and constructive action—music, poetry, art, as well as moral concern for justice, love, compassion, and righteousness. The *yetzer hara* is by contrast the innate drive for aggrandizement—the competitive instinct, greed, lust, and the temptation to succeed at any cost. This aggressive impulse, however, is not entirely negative or destructive. According to a midrash, it may even be channeled into positive directions. As the sages noted, "For were it not for the aggressive impulse (*yetzer hara*), no man would build a house, or marry a wife, nor beget children, nor engage in a trade" (Kohelet Rabbah 3:11).

Elsewhere in the midrash, the aggressive impulse is reduced almost to a neutral force that a person may then manipulate for good or evil purposes. A constructive application of that impulse will follow the proper observance of the Torah, as the midrash explains: "Like iron, out of which man can fashion whatever implements he pleases when he heats it in the forge, so the aggressive impulse can be subdued to the service of God if tempered by the words of Torah which is like fire" (*Avot of Rabbi Nathan,* Perek 16).

With this set of premises about the nature of the human condition, the rabbinic sages concluded that sin or wrongdoing was a state of action, not a state of being. They taught that Adam's disobedience in the garden of Eden was not the original sin that contaminated all future generations of humankind, but that it was a prototype, a paradigm, of the kind of transgression to which all people may succumb as a result of their own imperfections. The "fall" of

Adam is an object lesson in the inevitable limitations of finite creatures. The rabbis carefully emphasized the full responsibility of every individual for his/her own sin despite the effects of Adam's "fall."

Nowhere in its literature does Judaism require a person to atone for some burden of guilt inherited from the past, even though the Torah acknowledges (Exod. 20:5) that the errors of earlier generations invariably affect the predicament of later generations. No sacrifices in the ancient Temple at Jerusalem, however, were ever associated with an eternal transgression. No ceremonies or rituals even hinted at such a concept. Judaism also never embraced the hope that God would in some manner intervene in the affairs of a doomed humanity to remove the curse of this guilt from Adam's descendants and to redeem people from their presumably corrupt, evil nature.

In Jewish tradition, the sin of Adam did not extinguish human moral freedom or initiative. The major focus has always centered not on the origin of sin but on the avoidance of wrongdoing, and on ways to eliminate it. No person is condemned to sin; but all people are capable of it, simply because all people are endowed with free will and the power to choose between good and evil.

Jewish theology teaches that if a person has committed a sin, he/she may repent and be forgiven. The initiative, however, must come from the individual, not from God. The psalmist declared that "the LORD is near to all who call on Him . . . in truth" (Ps. 145:18). The prophet Malachi assured his listeners, "Return to me, and I will return to you, says the LORD of hosts" (Mal 3:7).

In Judaism the highest of virtues is repentance. No other religious literature is more explicit on the subject. The Talmud teaches that "in the place where a repentant sinner stands, even the righteous who have never sinned cannot stand" (*Berakhot* 34b). This comparison does not necessarily imply that repentant transgressors are better than the wholly righteous, but only that they occupy a very special place on a divine scale of values.

Furthermore, repentance in Judaism is not a mystery or a sacrament. It does not imply any miraculous transformations in the individual or the rebirth of his/her soul. Rather, repentance is largely a human undertaking. It involves a four-step process that begins with a readiness to acknowledge a wrongdoing, followed by acts of compensation for the injury inflicted and genuine resolve to avoid a repetition of the same sinful deed. Only then can a person continue with the fourth and final step of praying for forgiveness and cherish the expectation of receiving God's mercy.

In Jewish tradition, life is entirely a matter of choices. One may choose either good or evil. From the moment of birth every person is a free agent. One may sin, or one may avoid it. One surely is not perfect, but every person is perfectible; and one's purpose in life is to achieve as much of that moral potential as one's humanity will allow. The task is not to eliminate aggressive inclinations but to control them and channel them. A person can be all that God meant for him or her to be, or that person may ignore the opportunity. All depends on individual choice.

*Christianity.*    Christians believe that human beings were created in the image of God. To understand what it means to be human, then, one needs to understand something of the divine life. Christians believe that God's existence is marked by infinite, loving justice and that God is internally relational; that is, God is a Trinity of three coequal persons—Father, Son, and Holy Spirit—who live in such perfect cooperation and love that they are one God. Christians also believe that God is personal, not simply an impersonal force of nature, and rational, that God acts with intention. To say that humanity bears the image of God, then, means that human beings were created to live in loving, just relationships with one another. It also means that our capacity to think and act rationally is a crucial marker of our humanity and that true rationality is inseparable from love and justice.

To say that human beings bear the image of God, though, also highlights the fact that human beings are not God; they are creatures: finite, embodied, and mortal. Christianity affirms the fundamental goodness of creation. Because creation flows from the infinite goodness of God, it exists as the embodiment of God's goodness. Being human entails living as an embodied soul, as ensouled flesh, and this union of body and soul is both essential to our humanity and good. In other words, Christians celebrate the goodness of embodiment and reject the notion that the soul is trapped in the body from which it hopes to escape at death. Likewise, Christians do not accept the idea that souls can migrate from one body to another. To be human is to live an earthly life, body and soul. Christians extend this affirmation of the goodness of earthly life, body and soul, to their vision of redemption. Christians anticipate that when God's reign is fully come to earth, that the earth will be made new and that human beings will be raised from the dead to live bodily lives in joyous communion with God and one another.

Although Christians believe that humanity was created good, they also affirm that we have fallen from God's original intention for humanity so that we no longer live in loving, just relationships with one another, and our rationality no longer perfectly conforms to the standards of love and justice. Instead, we use our rational powers for destructive purposes and live in communities that do not display the love and justice God intended for humanity. Christian theology names this fall from God's intentions sin. Sin indicates two things for Christians. First, it names the particular ways and specific acts through which we violate the will of God. Second, sin indicates an underlying condition, a brokenness of the spirit, which expresses itself in particular sins. This underlying condition is known as original sin, a condition of separation from God shared by all people that prevents humanity from living as God intends. Sin leads to spiritual and physical death. Because of original sin all persons are in need of God's redeeming grace, even children who have not yet committed any actual or particular sins. Original sin is also, therefore, the origin of our particular sinful acts, which emerge from the underlying brokenness the way that a disease manifests itself in particular symptoms.

One theologian, Augustine, described original sin as a prideful rejection of our status as creatures. The first human beings, said Augustine, wanted to be gods and not creatures; they wanted to live for themselves, rather than living for the glory of God. When they rejected their status as creatures, they damaged the image of God in themselves with the result that they and all of their descendants now suffer from original sin.

The human condition, then, is one of living as the fallen image of God so that humanity suffers both spiritual and physical death. Christians affirm that in Christ, God works to redeem humanity so that we may live in conformity with God's will and in joyful communion with God and one another. Human salvation is achieved through the incarnation of Jesus Christ, whom Christians affirm to be perfect in humanity and perfect in divinity. Christians believe that in Jesus Christ God entered human existence in order to restore humanity to the image of God. Jesus Christ's life and death reconcile humanity to God so that we are no longer alienated, no longer subject to spiritual death. In Christ's resurrection from the dead, God overcomes even physical death so that humanity may live forever in the kingdom of God in joyful obedience and delightful communion.

***Islam.***    Islam celebrates the diversity that is found within humanity. Qur'an 49:13 states that the differences among people are ultimately a gift from God that enables us to learn about each other: "Oh, humanity! (God) has made you male and female, nations and tribes, so that you might know one another. Truly, the most noble among you in God's eyes is the most devout." The variety within human life should therefore be recognized as a God-given opportunity for growth and knowledge.

Despite that diversity, however, there is a firm belief in Islam that, at their core, all human beings are the same. As finite creatures that have been created by God, we all share the same basic human condition regardless of differences in gender, race, nationality, and religion. The thing that cuts through the distinctions among us is our complete dependence on God for our life and our survival. That reliance is vividly portrayed in the account of human origins in Qur'an 15:28–29, when God addresses the angels and tells them how humanity will be formed: "I am creating a human being from clay, formed mud. When I have fashioned him and breathed in him my spirit prostrate yourselves to him." God animates Adam, the first human being, with the breath of life that allows him to become a sensate, thinking person. This is the paradigm that explains how all subsequent humans are created.

Consequently, Islam teaches that all people are born muslims. Not Muslims, which designates those who follow the religion of the Prophet Muhammad, but muslims, in the sense of "submitters." Our birth is completely out of our control. We are each brought into existence by God, who breathes the spirit of life into us, and that divine act puts us in a position of submission whether we realize it or not. As we grow and mature, we can choose to reject or ignore our dependence on God, but that does not change the fact that we are muslims until the day we die. We constantly submit ourselves to the divine will because that is what it means to be a human being.

Islam does not teach that humanity fell from a perfect state and that the effects of that fall are passed on to succeeding generations. In other words, it does not ascribe to the notion of original sin that characterizes many Christian denominations. According to the Qur'an's version of the events in the garden, humanity disobeyed God, but that transgression did not lead to a change in the human condition. The account in Qur'an 7:22–25 picks up the story after Satan (not a serpent) has tricked the couple.

> Their Lord called out to them, saying, "Did I not forbid you to approach the tree, and did I not warn you that Satan is a clear enemy to you?" They said, "Our Lord, we have harmed ourselves. If you do not forgive us and have mercy on us we shall surely be among the lost." He said, "Go! Some of you will be enemies of each other. For a while, the earth will provide you a dwelling and life's necessities. There you shall live and there you shall die, and from there you shall be brought out."

The outcome of this version is different than what we find in Genesis 3:14–19. In the Bible the couple is punished and they are told they will die because of their disobedience. The Qur'an does not present such a bleak picture of the aftermath. Adam and Eve are the same people at the end of the text that they were at the beginning. They are expelled from the garden, but God does not curse them, and it seems that mortality has always been part of their human condition because they are not threatened with it in the Qur'an if they eat of the tree.

In the Muslim understanding, humans were created mortal with an innate capacity to do good. The first couple was tricked into disobeying, but that does not make them the first link in an unbroken chain of human sinfulness. If a Muslim sins, it is his or her fault and not the consequence of some primordial transgression. One of the most drawn-out and contentious debates within the Muslim community was that of free will vs. predestination. Are humans truly free to make their own decisions, or are all acts predetermined by God? Prominent intellectual heavyweights lined up on both sides of the issue, but it was eventually decided that humans are free and responsible for their own actions.

Islam's lack of belief in original sin means there is no preordained guilty condition from which humanity must be "saved." All people are born good, and it is up to each of us to make the proper choices as we exercise our free will. Muslims believe the surest way to do this is to submit one's own will to God's will as it is revealed to them through their religion.

## 2. How is the nature of God understood in the religion?

*Judaism.*    Ethical monotheism is a uniquely Jewish religious concept which affirms that all existence was created and is governed by a single God. That deity is also the source and paradigm for moral action. This idea was a revolutionary development in the history of religions. Many knowledgeable students of religion maintain that this proposition is the greatest single contribution of Judaism to the spiritual heritage of Western civilization.

This extraordinary understanding of the nature of God rests upon an appreciation of its three major aspects. The first is the belief that God is one and not many. The ancient Jewish people, unlike their contemporaries, did not believe that the world was fragmented under the domain of several different gods. They posited the existence of only one Supreme Being who alone accounted for all the diversity in the universe. This Being was the Creator and Sustainer of all there is. This first hypothesis implies several corollaries that emphasize the uniqueness of this concept.

One corollary entailed a belief that the unity of God encouraged much greater unity among the people who worshiped such a deity. If people worshiped many gods, favorites would inevitably emerge among them and factions would develop; each faction would promote the supremacy of its own choice. Monotheism theoretically precludes such conflicts. "In days to come," declares Isaiah, "the mountain of the LORD's house shall be established as the highest of the mountains. . . . Many peoples shall come and say: 'Come, let us go up to the mountain of the LORD, to the house of the God of Jacob; that he may teach us his ways, and that we may walk in his paths'" (Isa. 2:2–3). From its earliest beginnings Judaism taught that the unity of humankind was a corollary of the belief in one God. That is clearly a distinctive quality of the concept of monotheism.

When Judaism proclaims that God is one, it means that God is not simply a numerical unity, but also a qualitative unity. That is the second major aspect of monotheism in Judaism. God is not only one; God is unique as the Source and Sustainer of all moral values. God is not only one unto Himself; God is the only one of His kind in the universe. There is no other "One" like God. During the rabbinic period (200 BCE–500 CE), the Roman emperor often enjoyed the title of "king of kings." To emphasize the singularity of God, the rabbinic sages acclaimed God as "the King of the kings of kings."

To hold that God is the Source and Sustainer of moral values is to insist on an objective status for ethical ideals. They are not the impulsive fabrication of human minds but are grounded in the very bedrock of creation. Moral laws have objective validity similar to the laws of physics. They are not our invention, but it is for us to discover them. Just as it would be foolish to defy the law of gravity and hope to escape its consequences, so is it perilous to presume that a human infant can grow to emotional maturity without ever being loved or cared for. In both cases the penalty for ignoring the law is a natural consequence of defying the given realities of the universe. The uniqueness of God in this context is the complex but delicate blend of both physical and spiritual reality in a single deity that accounts for the balance, harmony, and order of nature within us and without.

The uniqueness of God, as Judaism has taught it, includes still a third aspect that clearly set ancient Israel apart from all other peoples. Evidence abounds that from earliest times God in Judaism was not simply the supreme moral authority but also the supreme moral agent. Because God limited God's range of operations by imposing particular moral laws, God's credibility henceforth would rest not only on legislating truth but on being identified with truth. God could not violate either physical or moral laws without seriously compromising God's own integrity.

A biblical passage that clearly reflects this principle is the conversation between God and Abraham concerning the impending destruction of Sodom and Gomorrah (Gen. 18:17–33). God decides to disclose to Abraham God's plans to destroy the two cities because of their flagrant transgressions of moral decency. Abraham, however, objects to such a decision that would indiscriminately obliterate the innocent with the guilty, and calls God to account on the basis of God's own ethical standards.

"Wilt thou indeed," asks Abraham, "destroy the righteous with the wicked?" He then proceeds to negotiate with God on behalf of the innocent. He begins by speculating whether there may be as few as fifty righteous people in the cities. Would that not be sufficient to annul the decree? God concedes that Abraham's argument is legitimate and agrees that for the sake of fifty righteous people the cities will be saved if Abraham can find them. Abraham proceeds to inquire for the sake of forty, then thirty, twenty, and finally just ten. In each case God is willing to alter God's judgment if the innocent numbers can be found.

Eventually, not even ten innocent people can be found, and God proceeds to destroy the cities. The point, however, is not Abraham's defeat but his acknowledged right to challenge God and hold God personally accountable for the laws God had commanded.

Ethical monotheism is not just a way of talking about God. It is a way of understanding human experience; it is a way of organizing the world in which we live. It is a faith that attempts to explain what we do not know by beginning with what we do know. We do know our awareness of this world is rooted in a unity of our own senses. We do know that defiance of moral law invites a disaster as devastating as any contempt for the laws of physics or chemistry or biology. We know, in short, that we cannot fathom it all and that this world is ultimately grounded in mystery. And that singular ethical mystery is what we call God.

*Christianity.*    God is understood, first of all, to be the one sovereign creator of all. God alone is infinite and eternal. God stands alone among all reality as God. Everything else that is real—living things and inert things, rational beings and the unintelligent, everything from the angels and human beings, to the animals and plants, to the planets, minerals, and elements—is a creature. All creatures owe their existence to God, whom they were made to glorify. The good of all creatures, therefore, is found in God, to whom they return in obedience and love.

The nature of the one, sovereign God who is creator of all is most essentially love. God is love. God's nature as love is communicated to creatures through God's goodness, beauty, mercy, and justice. These qualities all flow into creation because God wills other beings into existence out of nothingness and endows them with God's own qualities. The creation, then, is a finite and imperfect reflection of God's infinite and perfect love, goodness, and beauty.

The gap between what God is infinitely and what creation is in a finite way has led Christian theologians to the conclusion that our language about God never perfectly names what and who God is. Our language is a rough approximation of divine reality. It gestures us toward God without precisely capturing God's essence. We use analogies from the created order to indicate some truths about God, being careful not to confuse creator and creation. For instance, God is often referred to as the "rock of salvation," which points to God's steadfast faithfulness without identifying God with an inert mineral. Likewise, Christians call God "Father" to indicate God's loving, parental oversight of humanity, but do not assert that God is male. In fact, Christians have always insisted that God is neither male nor female.

The question of how precise our language can be in gesturing toward God has led to a debate among theologians about some of the attributes of God. The majority of theologians throughout Christian history have held that analogies from creation are always deeply flawed because they rest in some basic creational assumptions that do not apply to God. For instance, creatures are governed by time, but these theologians point out that God is eternal, which means that God exists outside of time. Likewise they affirm that God is immutable (changeless), omnipotent (all-powerful), and exists without needs of any kind. Many modern theologians, however, have questioned these classical attributes, claiming that the analogy between creation and God is much closer than the tradition has assumed. They claim, for instance, that God moves through time as creatures do, but never comes to an end. That is, they claim that God is everlasting, not eternal. These theologians also believe that God changes and responds through relationships with creatures and that God needs creatures so that God may live in loving relationship with others. They also believe that while God is very powerful, God is not all-powerful and cannot be held responsible for evil in the world. This debate remains unsettled, with both sides making faithful efforts to attend to the biblical witness and to human experience.

In addition to believing that God is one, sovereign, and loving, Christians also believe that God exists as a Trinity of three persons. Christians have always insisted that belief in the Trinity does not conflict with monotheism, but have often had trouble articulating precisely how this can be. The challenge has been to affirm that God is really one, but also really three. Some have proposed that God only appears to us as triune; that Father, Son, and Holy Spirit are but three names for different ways God is revealed to us. The church rejected this way of thinking about the Trinity at the first council of Constantinople in 381, the second ecumenical council.

Instead the church affirmed that Father, Son, and Holy Spirit are three persons who live in a perfect and permanent cooperative bond unlike any kind of creaturely unity because it exists outside of the limitations of space and time. A fourth-century theologian named Gregory of Nyssa explained that because creatures are united to one another only imperfectly and temporarily, two or more creatures never truly live as one. But the three persons of the Trinity always operate in perfect unity, and this perfection of unified operations ensures that the reality of being one God is as certain as the reality of being three persons. The three persons of the one God live a life of love, delight, and mutuality. Human beings may catch a glimpse of this delightful, loving triune life of God when they enter into relationships of love, reciprocity, and hospitality even though such relationships are always limited by our creaturely condition of being spatial and temporal.

There is one important point of disagreement about the nature of the Trinity between Eastern Orthodox Christians and Christians of the West. Eastern Christians affirm that the Father is the source of the unity of the Trinity. The Father begets the Son, and the Holy Spirit proceeds from the Father. It is important to remember that the acts of begetting and proceeding are not the same as creating. The Son and Holy Spirit are not creatures; they are coequal in godhead with the Father. Nevertheless, Eastern Christians affirm that in some mysterious way the Son is begotten and the Holy Spirit proceeds. Western Christians affirm these same truths except that they believe that the Holy Spirit proceeds from the Father *and the Son*. Augustine explained that the Holy Spirit is the bond of love between the Father and the Son, that the Holy Spirit proceeds from the Father and the Son as love. Eastern Christians, however, claim that this way of thinking about the Trinity reduces the Holy Spirit to an impersonal force who is not coequal in divinity with the Father and the Son. In the West, Christians follow the theology of Augustine and add the phrase "and the Son" to the Nicene Creed where it declares that the Holy Spirit proceeds from the Father. The Latin for this phrase "and the Son" is *filioque*, and the disagreement between East and West on this issue is sometimes known as the *filioque* controversy.

*Islam.*   The Arabic word *allah*, the standard Islamic term for God, translates literally as "the deity." It is not a personal name or title, but conveys more or less the same sense the English word "God" does. The defining quality of God's nature from the Muslim point of view is oneness, a view summed up succinctly in Qur'an 16:23: "Your God is one God." Neither of the other two monotheistic faiths places the emphasis on the unity and indivisibility of God that Islam does. The term for this aspect of God's nature is *tawhid*, which is etymologically related to the Arabic word for "one."

According to Islam, the worst thing a person can do is somehow to violate the unity of God. The term for this offense is *shirk*, which comes from an Arabic root that describes the act of associating or sharing something with something else. Someone guilty of this offense associates something from the

created world with the uncreated nature of God, thereby dividing up and denying the oneness that is the essence of the divine. This can be done physically,
by setting up an image or an idol as a sign of God, or intellectually, as when
one believes some individual or object shares in the divine nature. According
to the Qur'an, *shirk* is the greatest sin and the only offense that God cannot
forgive. "Truly, God will not forgive having something associated with him,
but he will forgive anything short of that as he pleases. Whoever associates
something with God has committed a very grave offense" (4:48).

This is the main reason that Islam does not permit paintings or other representations of God, a prohibition that is often extended to include images of
any living being. One of the most noticeable differences between a mosque
and many churches is that the former lacks any artwork depicting humans or
animals. This is avoided because such representations could be improperly
associated with God and therefore lead to *shirk*. The absence of such art is
also sometimes explained by the belief that only God has the right to create
living beings. The artist who produces such images is therefore guilty of trying to usurp God's power and authority. These views have not resulted in
mosques and other Islamic buildings that are devoid of all artwork. Rather,
they are typically adorned with very elaborate script and ornate geometric patterns like arabesque that are quite beautiful and aesthetically pleasing.

According to mainstream Muslim belief, God is a transcendent reality that
is ultimately unknowable to humanity. Despite that divide, there is a longstanding tradition in Islam that claims humans can know something about
God's nature even if we are incapable of grasping the totality of the divine
essence. Several times in the Qur'an, reference is made to the names of God:
"Allah—there is no God but he. To him belong the most beautiful names"
(20:8). These texts are the basis for a tradition that claims God has ninety-nine
names, each describing some aspect or quality of the deity. Many of these
names come from the Qur'an, and the list includes designations like the following: "the Highest," "the All-Seeing," "the Living," and "the Giver." Many
pious Muslims memorize the entire list of names or portions of it and recite
them in their personal prayers. In this way, they are able to know and reflect
on certain qualities that God possesses.

A final facet of the Muslim understanding of God deserving mention is the
belief that this is the same God worshiped by Jews and Christians. According
to the Qur'an, in various times and places throughout history God's word has
been revealed to prophets who were then charged with the task of communicating that message to their people. The names of many of these individuals
are familiar to Bible readers. Noah, Abraham, Moses, David, and Jesus, as
well as other biblical figures, are among those identified in the Qur'an as

prophets. This highlights an important belief about God's nature that Jews, Christians, and Muslims all share. As faiths that are based on revelation, they all maintain that God is an active conversation partner with humanity, even to the point of initiating contact with them in order to convey the divine will. Despite the radical monotheism of Islam that leads to a transcendent view of the deity as totally other, it teaches that God is deeply concerned about human beings and their destiny.

### 3. How is the relationship between God and humanity understood?

*Judaism.*  At every major turning point in Israel's history, the Jewish people encountered God in a different context. In the event of the exodus from Egypt, they discovered God as the sole protector and guarantor of human freedom. God was the spark of inspiration that compelled them to break the chains of slavery and to risk their lives and their children's lives for the precious, inalienable right to liberty. Only God can confer such a blessing. No human agent can bestow it or deny it.

At Sinai the Israelites envisioned God as the lawgiver, the source of every standard for justice, truth, and goodness. They discovered in their wilderness experience that the foundation of a stable society required rules that were rooted in some objective reality, not in the momentary impulse of popular fashion.

In their moments of trial and temptation they found in God their healer. In times of need, God became their helper. In the unfolding of an endless series of significant events they understood God as the author of history. Life was not a meaningless succession of unrelated accidents. The people of Israel assigned to their individual and collective lives a divine purpose that would ultimately lead to their own fulfillment and redemption.

Even in the face of total defeat God was their savior. For some people the defeat might mean death, and the salvation some form of life beyond the grave. In a larger context, however, the "defeat" might pertain to ignorance, insensitivity, fear, or any other human limitation. The victories a person achieves over these disabilities are clearly for Judaism a form of salvation or healing. This healing is also a display of God's power as a personal savior.

One of the outstanding contributors to the concept of God in Jewish tradition was the spiritual giant of Hellenistic Judaism, the philosopher Philo of Alexandria (30 BCE–45 CE). The influence of the traditional Jewish idea of God is clearly evident in the Philonic emphasis on God's transcendence and spirituality. The concept of God for Philo is elevated above all values and perfections conceivable to the human mind. God is above knowledge and virtue, even above the good and the beautiful. Since God is exalted above all that is knowable, only God's bare existence is accessible to our intellects. An attempt to blend Jewish and Hellenistic thought, Philo's aim essentially was to bring together and unify the two major categories of truth: human knowledge and divine revelation.

Any discussion of God's relationship to humankind in Judaism requires at least a brief reference to the concept of "the covenant." The covenant is simply an agreement between God and the Jewish people, the content of which is fully contained in the Torah, the first five books of the Hebrew Scriptures. The Covenant stipulates that God will protect and prosper the Jewish people, if they in return will observe the statutes and injunctions that God commands. If they violate those commandments, God will punish them. That the community of Israel is party to this difficult and divine partnership confers upon it the distinction of being a "chosen people." That "chosen-ness" implies primarily a heritage not of special privilege but of special responsibility, which serves as a unique model, a high standard of truth and goodness.

The belief that God actually chose the Jewish people for this task is a matter of faith. History, however, confirms that Israel chose God in these terms. That truth is what matters most of all. The Jewish people have forever perceived themselves as living to serve the Supreme Creator and have ascribed meaning and significance to their own experience only as a consequence of this imperishable relationship.

The limits of God's reality in the world and God's relationship to humankind in Judaism are defined only by the limits of human experience. Judaism teaches that God relates to people in as many ways as people choose to relate to God.

*Christianity.*    Two theological themes held in balance characterize the relationship between God and humanity. The first is the idea that creation is formed out of nothing; God did not draw on some preexistent matter when God made everything that exists. In sovereign power, God called forth creatures from nothingness. Creatures exist, therefore, sheerly by the gracious will of God. This means that God's existence is fundamentally different from creaturely existence. God is essentially unknowable to humanity because God's nature is beyond our capacity to grasp. The second theological theme is that of revelation; in spite of God's essential unknowability, God makes certain divine truths accessible to humanity. God is revealed to humanity through nature, the grandeur of which points to its creator, and through God's mighty acts in history, which are recorded in Scripture. But God is revealed especially through the incarnation, through Jesus Christ. Human beings, then, are related to God as creator and redeemer, but also as the unknowable one who is made known in Christ.

In the first place, then, the relationship between God and humanity is understood as the relationship between creator and creature. The first chapter of Genesis, the first book of the Christian canon, offers an account of the creation of human beings. It explains that God created humanity by speaking. God said, "'Let us make humankind in our image, according to our likeness'" (1:26), and God gave them "'dominion over the fish of the sea and over the birds of the air and over every living thing that moves upon the earth'" (1:28). This narrative sounds two important themes about what it means to be human in relation to God. Human beings are, first and foremost, creatures of God, called forth out of nothing at a word from God. Human beings depend utterly on God for having come into being and continue to rely on God to be sustained in existence. But human beings occupy a peculiar place in the created order. They are made in the image of God and given a special role, that of dominion, with respect to other creatures. Human beings are not God, are not of ultimate significance, but they are exalted creatures, worthy of being called the image of God, and entrusted with the care of other living things. Psalm 8 expresses it this way:

> When I look at your heavens, the work of your fingers,
>    the moon and the stars that you have established;
> what are human beings that you are mindful of them,
>    mortals that you care for them?
> Yet you have made them a little lower than God,
>    and crowned them with glory and honor.
> You have given them dominion over the works of your hands"
>                                             (8:3–6a)

In the second place, the relationship between God and humanity is understood as the relationship between redeemer and redeemed. Genesis goes on to explain that, in spite of their exalted place in creation, human beings reject the limited place God provides for them and sinfully seek to usurp the role of God. The condition of sin means that the image of God has become distorted in humanity and that human beings can no longer relate to God and one another as God intends. In sin, humanity turns its dominion over other creatures into domination. In Christ, therefore, God enters the human condition, restoring the image of God, and redeeming humanity from its sinful condition.

*Islam.* The name of the religion and the term used to designate someone who adheres to it capture very well the essence of Islam's understanding of the relationship between God and humanity. The word *islam* means "submission," and the *muslim* is a submitter, or one who engages in *islam*. The thing to which a Muslim submits is the will of God as it is revealed in the text of the Qur'an and the teachings of the faith. The individual believer must therefore always adopt an attitude of obedience and surrender before the power and majesty of God. At the same time, despite this position of inferiority, humanity also has a special role to play by virtue of the fact that God has placed it in a position of authority over the rest of creation.

These two aspects of the divine/human relationship can be neatly summed up in two images: human beings are simultaneously God's servants and God's representatives. On the one hand, because we are called to submit ourselves fully to the divine will our relationship with God most closely resembles that between a master and a servant. Just as the servant does the bidding of his or her master with no questions asked, so, too, should the Muslim respond to the will and desire of the deity. The relationship is not one of negotiation or compromise, but one of complete compliance.

This notion is conveyed quite well in the Arabic term most commonly used for worship, *'ibada*, which comes from a root that carries with it a sense of servitude or enslavement. An act of worship in Islam—be it prayer, fasting, making the pilgrimage, or anything else—is best understood as an expression of one's status as a servant to God's will. This same idea is reflected in one of the most common elements found in personal names in the Arabic-speaking Muslim world. The word *'abd*, which is etymologically related to *'ibada*, means "servant, slave." This word is often found in combination with terms and titles that refer to God, thereby identifying the bearer of the name as a servant of the deity. For example, the name Abdullah, literally "servant of Allah," is a very frequent personal name. Similarly, a name like Abd al-Rahman, meaning "servant of the Merciful One," draws on one of the ninety-nine names of God mentioned above. Such terminology reflects the core of the way Muslims see themselves before God.

At the same time, human beings are also God's representatives on earth. This can be seen in the account of the creation of humanity found in Qur'an 2:28–39, where God speaks to the angels and refers to Adam as a deputy or successor. The word found here is *khalifa*, which is the same term that is translated as "caliph" to describe those who rule the Muslim community in the place of the Prophet Muhammad after his death. The passage seems to be saying that humanity somehow acts as God's envoy in creation, and that the deity has endowed us with a certain duty that we are to exercise responsibly. This text is often cited to explain how humanity has a special status vis-à-vis the rest of the created order. According to this reading, we are meant to be God's agents in creation, and we should therefore be responsible stewards of what has been entrusted to us. But we must never make the mistake of assuming that our unique place in the world makes us closer to God or God's equals. Orthodox Islam is quite clear in its belief that a wide gulf separates humanity from the deity.

But some Muslims have maintained that the gulf can be crossed. Sufis, like the mystics in other religions, believe it is possible to have a profound personal experience of God. They base this view on certain traditions of the Prophet Muhammad, whose strict ascetic lifestyle allowed him to know God intimately, and on texts of the Qur'an that appear to challenge the idea that humans can never truly know God. One of the most famous passages is 50:16, which states that God is closer to a person than his or her jugular vein. Sufis cite such texts as evidence that it is possible to grow closer to God, some even arguing that the believer and the deity can eventually become one. The Sufi masters and schools have devised various means, such as chanting and dancing, that allow the individual to come to experience the unity of all creation in God despite the apparent multiplicity that we perceive. The whirling dervishes who follow the disciplines established by the famous poet and mystic Jalaludin Rumi (1207–73) are one such group. Many of the ideas espoused by Sufism run counter to more traditional Muslim views regarding the relationship between God and humanity. Nonetheless, it has always been recognized as a valid and legitimate expression of Islamic faith.

Chapter Six

# Practices

## 1. Where is the main place of worship?

*Judaism.* After the destruction of the First Commonwealth in 70 CE, the synagogue replaced the Temple as the primary place for worship in Jewish life. The synagogue originated probably in Babylonia after the fall of Judea in 586 BCE. The Diaspora community there created an extraordinary spiritual and intellectual movement that included a new form of worship destined to become a paradigm for all Western religion. The central feature was the reading of Holy Scripture. The explanation of that Scripture was then added in order that the people might understand and appreciate its message, a methodology that eventually became the sermon. Prayers, hymns, and psalms gave voice to the yearning and hope of a community in exile. This common pattern of religious worship was a gift of Judaism to the Western world.

Those who joined together for this purpose in common search for God became a "synagogue," a gathering. The synagogue was not a physical structure and thus could not be destroyed. Indeed, the institution has remained immune to the ravages of time and the attacks of enemies, even though many synagogue buildings have been reduced to ashes. This place of meeting, wherever it had existed, had acquired the name of those who met there: the gathering, or the synagogue.

The synagogue edifice itself followed the structural divisions of the Temple in Jerusalem. The ancient Temple contained three major compartments, which included the courts where the people assembled, the sanctuary where the priests performed their sacred functions, and the Holy of Holies behind the curtain where the Ark that housed the Tablets of the Ten Commandments rested. The Temple courts were transformed into the people's gathering place; the sanctuary became the space where the prayer leader led the people in worship and offered their petitions to God. The holy of holies was replaced by the

84

Ark, the *Aron Kodesh*, in which the Torah scroll resided. Very often a curtain covered the Ark as it did the Holy of Holies.

This plan of a sacred meeting place therefore originated with Jewish practice. Only Judaism in the ancient world constructed meeting halls for the people; the other temples of antiquity elsewhere were small physical structures, abodes of the gods from which ordinary people were excluded. Judaism made religious observance democratic.

The words *synagogue* and *temple* are virtually interchangeable. Neither are Hebrew terms. *Synagogue* comes from the Greek meaning "bringing together," and *temple* comes from the Latin *templum*. A generation or more ago "temple" referred usually to a Reform or Conservative structure, while "synagogue" referred to an Orthodox house of worship. Today, however, those distinctions hardly apply. In some communities the temple may be Conservative while the Reform congregation is called a synagogue.

As the Greek term suggests, a synagogue is more than a place of prayer. It is a gathering place—the focal point for all Jewish communal life. In addition to being a sanctuary for worship, it serves also as a place of Jewish learning, education, and youth activities. It is also a place for general assembly as well as for social activities. For many centuries in many places the synagogue even served as a hostel for travelers and visitors.

Some synagogues were originally called temples, because they were established almost exclusively as a house of prayer. As time altered its function, however, the word expanded in meaning. A Jewish temple today, like the synagogue, is synonymous with the entire range of religious, cultural, and social services of a congregation. In addition, a synagogue nowadays may number its members in the thousands of people, or it may be as small as a minyan of ten individuals, or a *havurah* of several families or single men and women.

The major symbols of the synagogue are as old as the faith itself. In most synagogues the most conspicuous symbol placed over the Ark is either the tablets containing the first two words of each of the Ten Commandments or an inscription from biblical or rabbinic literature that reflects a cardinal precept of Judaism.

Every synagogue also displays a seven-branched candelabrum, the menorah. This ceremonial object first appeared in the sanctuary in the wilderness, described in the book of Exodus. According to legend, when Solomon built the Temple in Jerusalem, ten tall imposing golden candelabra stood in the central hall of worship in remembrance of the biblical menorah.

The eternal light, *ner tamid*, which hangs before the Ark, also predates the Temple of Solomon. Originally an oil lamp, but now often electrified in most sanctuaries, the oil lamp is never extinguished but symbolizes the continuity of Jewish observance through time as well as the eternal presence of God.

Most modern synagogues also use other symbols, largely for decorative purposes. Frescoes and murals usually depict festival and holy day symbols, such as the shofar, the megillah, the palm branch, or scenes from biblical narratives. The lions of Judah are also a favorite aesthetic symbol.

*Christianity.*    Because God is understood as creator of all, and all things are understood to exist for the glory of God, any place can provide the setting for Christian worship. But most Christians gather for regular weekly worship in a space specifically designated for that purpose. The building where worship is conducted is sometimes called a "church," though this term more properly applies to the gathering itself. Within the church building one room, called the sanctuary or nave, is usually set apart for the gathering. In traditions such as Roman Catholicism and Eastern Orthodoxy the worship space is understood to be holy in a way that makes it fundamentally different from any other space. In most Protestant traditions the worship space is treated with great respect because of the function it serves, but, since all of creation is understood to be holy, it is not fundamentally different from other spaces. Some Protestants signify this by referring to the church building simply as the "meeting house."

The worship space is typically divided into three areas. The first is an anteroom called the narthex that serves as a place of preparation. The narthex serves both a practical and a spiritual function. It provides a buffer between the outside world and the room where the community worships, allowing worshipers to prepare themselves to enter the worship space without distraction. The narthex may provide coat rooms, for example, or literature about the ministries of the congregation. The narthex also provides worshipers a space where they can prepare themselves spiritually for worship, centering their thoughts on the purposes of worship and quieting concerns that might distract them from those purposes.

The narthex leads into the main worship space, the nave. Except in Eastern Orthodox churches, this space is also called the sanctuary. The nave may contain pews or chairs where worshipers sit during the service, kneelers for use during prayers, Bibles, prayer books, and hymnals. In some traditions it will be lavishly decorated with stained glass windows depicting scenes from the Bible, icons of saints, statuary, and banners and paraments related to the season of the church year. In other traditions, especially among some Protestants, the nave will be very plain, with whitewashed walls and clear windows. The tradition of plainer naves began among some of the Protestant Reformers who were convinced that the Bible did not provide warrant for the use of images in church and who believed that such lavish decorations might distract the faithful from the worship of God. Those traditions that include images in worship have argued that the created order points us toward its creator and may properly be represented in church. Most churches will have a cross hanging somewhere near the front of the nave.

At the front of the nave, and usually elevated by a few steps, is a third area, the chancel. It contains a table or altar for communion, a Bible, a pulpit for preaching and reading, sometimes a lectern, a font or pool of water used for baptism, and perhaps a choir loft. There are also chairs used by worship leaders. In many churches a low railing may separate the chancel from the rest of the nave. In Eastern Orthodox churches, the arrangement differs. A screen of icons physically and visually separates the nave from the communion table. The space containing the communion table is referred to as the sanctuary, and only priests may enter it.

Christian worship varies widely. Some churches do not use instrumental music; others do not provide seating; some use kneelers while others do not; some make use of icons while others forbid them. Regardless of the type of space used or the style of worship, nearly every Christian church includes objects associated with the means of grace: a pulpit for reading and proclaiming the Word, a table or altar for communion, and a font or pool for baptism. These means of grace unite the church and influence the kinds of spaces Christians make use of in worship.

*Islam.*    The mosque is the Islamic equivalent of the Jewish synagogue and the Christian church. It is the location where organized communal prayer takes place, and it is the building the local Muslim community most closely identifies with its faith. The two Arabic words commonly used for the mosque are *masjid* and *jami'*, each of which gets at some aspect of what takes place within its walls. *Masjid* means "place of prostration," an allusion to the bending over and bowing that are the characteristic physical movements of Muslim prayer. The word *jami'* comes from a root that carries the primary sense of gathering and joining together, thereby identifying the mosque as the place where the members of the community assemble to express their shared faith.

Many mosques, particularly large ones, have an open courtyard that is enclosed on all sides by a covered walkway. This area is a place for people to meet and socialize, and it usually contains a space that is reserved for performing the obligatory ablutions prior to prayer. Muslims must be in a state of physical and spiritual purity when praying, and there is a series of carefully prescribed washing rituals that one must undertake before entering the mosque. It is forbidden for anyone, including tourists and visitors, to wear shoes in a mosque, so there is always a place near the doorway to store footwear.

Certain architectural features are found in every mosque. Muslims must pray facing Mecca, and the mihrab is a niche in the wall that indicates the direction toward the holy city. It is usually in the form of a doorway or an archway that is recessed into the wall but is not an actual opening. Very large mosques that can hold thousands of people will sometimes have more than one mihrab, but one of them is usually considered the primary one, and it is larger and more ornate than the others. The mihrab can be very simple and unadorned, but it is often decorated with elaborate geometric patterns and inscriptions, usually texts from the Qur'an.

To the right of the mihrab is the *minbar*, or pulpit, another standard feature of a mosque that goes back to the time of the Prophet Muhammad. The *minbar* is a raised platform that is reached by a series of steps, and there is often a door at the base of the steps. It is also common to find a dome or canopy over the platform at the top of the staircase. This is the location from which the sermon is delivered during noon prayers on Friday, the most important prayer time of the week. The *minbar* is usually made of either stone or wood, and those of wood tend to be more elaborately decorated with carvings, inscriptions, and inlaid elements.

The minaret is another architectural feature that is identified with mosques. This is a tower-like structure that is usually attached to the main building from which the call to prayer is proclaimed. In earlier periods the *muezzin*, whose job it is to call people to prayer, would climb the steps of the minaret and deliver the call five times a day. This is still the case at some mosques, but with the rise of modern technology it is more common today to hear a recording of the call to prayer. The minaret is not an essential element of mosque architecture, and it did not become a standard part of the design until the beginning of the Abbasid period in 750.

Those who are accustomed to churches and synagogues as places of worship are often quite surprised when they enter a mosque for the first time because there are no pews or seats. They find themselves in a large open area without any furniture that is broken up by pillars or columns. Lamps adorn the walls and hang from the ceiling, and the entire floor is covered with carpets. One's attention is not immediately drawn to one location or direction because there is no altar or ark containing the sacred text. A mosque does not contain a sacred space that can be accessed by only a few and is off limits to the rest of the community. Any Muslim is free to stand in or touch any part of a mosque.

In most mosques men and women pray separately. Sometimes there is a balcony for the women, and elsewhere there is a partition between them and the men. In some mosques there is a separate room where the women gather to pray. In a few places, especially in the West, men and women pray together in the same space.

Muslims are required to go to the mosque only for noon prayers on Friday. For the other thirty-four prayer times of the week they are free to pray wherever they wish as long as they face toward Mecca and follow the prescribed ritual. This means that just about any place in the world can become a *masjid*, or place of prostration. It is not uncommon to see a Muslim unroll a prayer rug and begin to pray in public when the call to prayer is heard.

## 2. What are the primary rituals and practices of the religion?

*Judaism.*    From the moment he awakens until the time he retires, an observant Jew fills his day with words of gratitude to God. He recites a blessing for washing his hands and face, for setting foot on the floor, for attending to his bodily needs, and for dressing in his customary garments. Women are generally exempted from these obligations, in part because Judaism originated in a patriarchal, Oriental culture, but also in large measure because the sages deliberately excused women as homemakers from all positive commandments in which the time for observance was a determining factor.

An observant Jew may invoke God's name repeatedly, because benedictions are assigned to almost every conceivable waking experience, such as eating between meals, sitting down to study Torah, purchasing and wearing a new garment, beginning a journey, tasting a new fruit, seeing lightning, hearing thunder, watching the ocean, observing a rainbow, or noticing trees beginning to blossom in the spring. A blessing exists even for meeting a person who is learned in Torah or general studies, for hearing good news, or for absorbing bad news. In addition every person is expected to devote a portion of each day to study, either privately or as a student in class.

One of the central enduring rituals of Judaism is kashrut ("ritual fitness"). Kashrut technically refers not only to properly prepared foods but to ritual objects of any kind. A Torah scroll may or may not be *kasher*/kosher ("ritually fit") depending on its composition and its condition. The same principle applies to a prayer shawl, an eternal light, or a mezuzah (a small encased scroll attached to the doorpost of a Jewish home).

In its application to food, kashrut is based on biblical injunctions about prohibited foods that are detailed in Leviticus 11 and Deuteronomy 14. All vegetables and fruits are permitted. In other categories, prohibited meats include the flesh of all animals such as horses and pigs whose hooves are not cloven and that do not chew the cud. Only fish with fins and scales are permitted, which therefore excludes all shellfish. Fowl that are "unclean" because they are birds of prey are not kosher.

Even ritually permissible foods must be slaughtered in a carefully prescribed manner by a person who is licensed for that purpose and is known as a *shochet* ("ritual slaughterer"). Carcasses of kosher animals may not reveal any trace of serious disease, especially in the lungs. They must also be drained of blood; this is accomplished by the slaughtering method and by soaking and salting the meat before it is cooked. Furthermore, according to Talmudic law, meat and meat products may not be prepared, served, or eaten with milk products or milk derivatives. Utensils and dishes that belong to one category may not be mixed with those of the other. A person must even wait a specific period of time between consuming portions of meat and milk products.

Whatever is forbidden according to the categories of kashrut is termed *terefah*, which in Hebrew means literally "torn" and referred originally to any living animal that had fallen victim to a beast or bird of prey and was therefore unacceptable as a food. Eventually, the concept of *terefah* extended to all forbidden foods.

Jewish tradition also emphasizes the observance of *mikveh*. *Mikveh* is a process of immersion in water from a continually fresh, flowing source for purposes of ritual purification. This observance became not only the paradigm for later Christian baptism, but endured as a prerequisite in Judaism for ritual purity from earliest antiquity. Archaeological findings confirm *mikveh* as one of the most ancient of all Jewish rituals.

Originally, only Orthodox women attended the *mikveh*, primarily to regain ritual purity after the menstrual period. In our time, however, *mikvaot* (plural) exist in countless Jewish communities and attract both men and women for a wide range of spiritually significant moments, including recovery from illness or addictions of various kinds, anniversaries, graduations, preparation for marriage, closure for divorce, or even preparation for Shabbat. Once reserved for Orthodox believers, *mikveh* now caters to many non-Orthodox Jews as well.

One of the fundamental rituals of Jewish observance is the ceremony of Brit Milah, from the Hebrew meaning the "covenant of circumcision." Circumcision began with Abraham (Gen. 17:10–27) as the seal of the covenant between him and God. It transformed Abraham into a Jew. Ever since that time all male children are bound by the same ritual.

Just as male infants are named at their circumcision, female children are named in a comparable ceremony called *b'rit chayim*, the "covenant of life," which occurs either at home or in the synagogue. If held in the synagogue the ceremony may include an *aliyah* ("calling up") to the Torah for the parents of the child, during which time they also offer a special blessing for their daughter.

The thirteenth year was a significant milestone in the life of every young Jewish boy. To celebrate the completion of his total reliance on others for his moral and intellectual growth, and the beginning of his own accountability in that enterprise, he was called to recite the blessings over the Torah on the Sabbath immediately following his thirteenth birthday. Sometime in the Middle Ages, the custom evolved of designating a young man at this stage of life as a bar mitzvah, from the Hebrew meaning literally "a son of the commandment," but more freely signifying "a responsible Jew."

In contemporary Reform and Conservative Judaism this ritual also includes girls. In most cases the ceremony is exactly the same or very similar, except that for girls it is called a bat mitzvah, from the Hebrew meaning "a daughter of the commandment."

*Christianity.* A Christian service of worship incorporates many of the most important rituals for the faith. Sunday services will include readings from Scripture, a sermon, prayers, a collection of funds taken up for the poor and to support the ministries of the church, sacred music, and the celebration of sacraments. Sacraments are among the most important of Christian practices. Together with the hearing of Scripture they are understood as means of grace, means through which God graciously works in human life. A sacrament is often defined as outward and visible sign of an inward and spiritual grace. Christians believe that God acts through the material elements of the sacrament (the outward and visible sign) to bring individuals to faith and to sustain them in that faith. The two sacraments universally acknowledged by Christians are baptism and the Lord's Supper.

Baptism is the sacrament of initiation that marks one as a member of the church, as a subject of God's redeeming grace. At its heart, baptism is a rite of washing, so the material element associated with baptism is water, which signifies the washing away of sin. The name of the Holy Trinity is pronounced as a candidate for membership is washed with water. Sometimes this washing takes the form of full-body immersion in a pool of water; at other times, water is poured or sprinkled on a candidate's head. A candidate for baptism will renounce evil and profess faith in Christ prior to receiving the sacrament or, in the case of an infant, a parent or sponsor will make these renunciations and affirmations for the child. Christians disagree about whether baptism is appropriate for infants and others unable to confess faith.

The majority of Christians advocate for infant baptism because it is believed that God works through baptism to confer faith. Others advocate for believer's baptism because they believe that the sacrament does not confer faith but instead declares the presence of faith. Because belief and practice are closely linked in the Christian faith, baptism is always accompanied by a process of education. In the case of believer's baptism, a process of education may be undertaken in preparation for receiving the sacrament. In the case of infant baptism, the parents and congregation take a vow to guide and nurture the child in faith.

Whereas baptism is the sacrament associated with receiving redeeming faith and is received only once in a lifetime, the Lord's Supper is the sacrament that sustains the faithful and is received many times throughout a Christian's life. The Lord's Supper is a shared meal of bread and wine, and these material elements signify the body and blood of Christ, which was broken and spilled for human salvation. The sacrament begins when the faithful are invited to come to the table to commune with Christ. A prayer of thanksgiving is offered and words of institution are pronounced. The words may be part of the prayer or may be said alone after the prayer. The words call the faithful to remember that on the night Christ was arrested, he shared a meal of bread and wine with his disciples and commanded them to remember his broken body whenever they shared bread and his spilled blood whenever they shared the cup. All baptized members then partake of the elements and conclude the sacrament with another prayer of thanksgiving. Christians affirm that, through the sacrament, Christ is present with believers, strengthening and sustaining them. For this reason the sacrament is sometimes called "communion," since Christ communes with the faithful through it. Many Christians, including Eastern Orthodox, Roman Catholics, and many Lutherans and Anglicans/Episcopalians affirm that the body of Christ is literally present in the sacrament. Others affirm the spiritual presence of Christ in the sacrament.

In addition to these two sacraments, Roman Catholics include five others. In the sacrament of confirmation children confirm the vows that were made for them in baptism and are eligible to begin receiving the Lord's Supper. The sacrament of reconciliation, also known as confession, calls believers to repent of their sins and to engage in acts of penitence in preparation for receiving the Lord's Supper. The sacrament of anointing is for those who are ill or suffering. It is practiced especially as a Christian nears death and is sometimes known as "last rites" or "extreme unction." The sacrament of holy orders is for those ordained to the priesthood or consecrated to monastic life, and the sacrament of matrimony is for those who join their lives together in marriage.

*Islam.*    Islam is a religion of orthopraxy, or proper action. In such a faith, it is not enough to hold certain beliefs. It is equally important that those beliefs be expressed through one's actions. How you put your faith into action and live your life ultimately determine whether or not you are a true Muslim. The core practices of Islam are referred to as the "five pillars." All Muslims are expected to demonstrate their faith by doing these five things: profess the faith, pray, give alms, fast, and make the pilgrimage to Mecca.

The Muslim profession of faith is quite brief and simple, especially when compared to certain Christian creeds. It is a statement consisting of two parts: "I testify that there is no God but God, and that Muhammad is God's messenger." In order to become a Muslim, someone with an understanding of the faith and the proper intent need only recite those words. There is no formal ceremony or ritual that signals one's membership in the *ummah.* The profession of faith is also heard throughout the course of every day in Islamic countries because it is part of the call to prayer. In this way, Muslims are constantly reminded of two of the essential elements of their religion: its monotheism and its prophet.

Muslims are expected to pray every day at five prescribed times that are determined by the position of the sun in the sky: dawn, noon, mid-afternoon, sunset, and evening. After performing ablutions during which the hands, mouth, face, and feet are washed, they turn toward Mecca and follow precise rubrics to fulfill their obligation. The *rak'a*, a word related to the Arabic verb "to bow down," is the basic unit of prayer. Each *rak'a* starts with the phrase "God is great," and includes bows, prostrations, prayers, and brief Qur'an texts. Each *rak'a* takes only a few minutes to complete and, depending on the time of day, between two and four of them must be completed.

The third pillar is almsgiving. All Muslims should give a portion of their accumulated wealth to the community to provide for its upkeep and assist those in need. This money is usually used to help the poor and those who work with them, to contribute toward education and outreach programs, and to support the building and maintenance of mosques. The standard amount to be given is 2.5 percent of one's assets. Some Islamic countries have a ministry that is in charge of collecting and managing these funds, but in most places donations are strictly voluntary and are not required by law.

During Ramadan, the ninth month of the year, all Muslims are required to fast from dawn until dusk. Islamic tradition associates the Ramadan fast with the beginning of the revelations received by the Prophet Muhammad. Only mature adults who are physically able to carry out this obligation are required to do so. The sick, pregnant and nursing women, or those traveling great distances do not have to fast, but they should make up for the missed days as soon as they can. During this month Muslims must refrain from food, drink, smoking, and sexual activity during daylight hours. The setting of the sun begins the *iftar*, the breaking of the fast when families get together for prayers and a common meal. Islam's use of a lunar calendar means that Ramadan is not fixed during one season of the year. In years when it occurs during the summer, the fast presents many hardships and challenges, particularly for Muslims who work outdoors.

The final pillar is the pilgrimage to Mecca that is required of all Muslims who are able to afford it and can physically make the trip. It entails completing a series of set rituals over a week's time in and around the city of Mecca during the first half of the twelfth month of the year. Millions of Muslims from all over the world participate in these ceremonies every year, and those who successfully complete them are given the title hajj, or pilgrim, indicating their new status.

There are, of course, many other activities and devotional practices that Muslims engage in, but these five are important because they are shared by all and they constitute the ritual framework of the faith. Each of them traces its roots back to the earliest period of the faith, and each is mentioned in the Qur'an and the hadith. Finally, the many similarities among the practices within the three monotheistic faiths should be noted as an opportunity for interreligious dialogue and understanding. Jews, Christians, and Muslims share much in common by virtue of the fact that they all profess their faith, pray, give alms, fast, and visit holy places.

## 3. What are the important holidays and celebrations throughout the year?

*Judaism.*    The most important of all Jewish holy days is Shabbat, the Sabbath. The Sabbath is the only holiday that is prescribed by the Ten Commandments. It is a weekly period of recreation and restoration. Part of its purpose is religious commitment, but part is also social responsibility. It is both a reminder of creation, according to Exodus 20:11, and a reenactment of emancipation and a celebration of freedom, as proclaimed in Deuteronomy 5:15. The gift of the Sabbath is a unique contribution of Judaism to humankind. The entire body of social legislation in the Western world is based on it. For the Jewish people the Sabbath is the supreme symbol of the covenant between God and themselves.

The Sabbath is not a day of gloom or sorrow; to the contrary it is a time for joy and delight. It is a time devoted to worship, learning, reading, thoughtful reflection in the company of family and friends, and refreshing leisure that enhances the quality of ordinary living, such as a brisk walk on the beach, a stroll through the woods, a swim in the lake, or a hike in the mountains. It may be a time for visiting the sick, the lonely, the bereaved. It is even time for a quiet, restful nap, which the sages termed "a delight." As in Judaism generally, so on Shabbat specifically, earthly pleasures were never excluded from the realm of spirituality.

The first ten days of the Hebrew calendar are known collectively as the Ten Days of Repentance. It is a very solemn period, a time for serious reflection and self-assessment. These days begin on the first day of the month of Tishri, which is Rosh Hashanah, the "New Year," and culminate on the tenth day, Yom Kippur, or the "Day of Atonement." These are such eminently sacred occasions for renouncing transgressions and seeking divine forgiveness that Jews address them as the High Holy Days. Indeed, Yom Kippur is the only holy day that even supersedes the Sabbath in importance, which is why it is frequently called "the Sabbath of Sabbaths."

The Hebrew calendar includes the celebration of three major festivals, namely, Sukkot (Tabernacles), *Pesach* (Passover), and Shavuot (Pentecost). Originally all were agricultural feast days marking the completion of a harvest period. They were also called pilgrim festivals, because they included the requirement of a pilgrimage to the Temple at Jerusalem as a display of thanksgiving for the bountiful blessings God had provided. In the course of time each of these festivals also developed a primary association with a climactic event in the history of the Jewish people. Thus Sukkot became synonymous with the wanderings through the wilderness, *Pesach* with the emancipation from bondage in Egypt, and Shavuot with the theophany (revelation) at Sinai.

The Torah designates the first and last days of Sukkot and *Pesach* (the first and last two days in Conservative and Orthodox Judaism) as "holy convocations" that preclude any ordinary labor but specify a particular liturgy for observing the festival. Among traditionally observant Jews, Shavuot is celebrated for two days instead of one and is also a "holy convocation."

The calendar cycle of holidays in Judaism also includes a series of minor festivals. They are considered minor not because they are necessarily less meaningful than other holidays, but primarily because they do not include any special liturgies or the major categories of prohibited activities associated with other festivals.

Probably the two most significant holidays in this category are Hanukkah and Purim. Hanukkah is the first recorded battle in history for freedom of conscience. The name of the festival means "education" or "dedication." It refers not so much to the military victory of the Maccabees over the Greek-Syrian tyranny but to the rededication of the Temple, which had been defiled by the enemy as a pagan shrine. Hanukkah focuses far more on the triumph of right-eousness than on the triumph of armed might. The most fitting summation of its message is the statement from the haftarah (prophetic portion) assigned for the Sabbath during the holiday that proclaims, "Not by might, nor by power, but by my spirit, says the LORD of hosts" (Zech. 4:6).

Just as Hanukkah celebrates the first successful struggle for the survival of Judaism, the festival of Purim represents the first successful struggle for the survival of the Jewish people. *Purim* is the Hebrew term for "lots" and refers to the method by which the date was chosen to destroy the Jews of ancient Persia.

The story of Purim is based on the biblical narrative in the book of Esther. Even though the tale is more fiction than fact, subsequent historical events cer-tainly substantiated the belief that the Purim episode is a paradigm of the threats and mortal dangers that have assailed the Jewish people in every gen-eration. The joyous conclusion in the book of Esther was a constant beacon of hope and encouragement in the darkest and most dismal of times.

*Christianity.*    The most important day for Christians is Sunday, the first day of the week. This is the day when Christians gather for worship and to remem-ber and celebrate Christ's resurrection. The whole gospel is celebrated each Sunday. Nevertheless, over the centuries Christians have developed an annual cycle of seasons and holidays to commemorate central events in the life of Christ and the establishment of the church. This "church calendar" allows Christians to mark time in a way distinct from the secular calendar that begins on January 1. The church year, which varies slightly among traditions, con-sists of a Christmas cycle followed by a season of ordinary time and then an Easter cycle followed by another season of ordinary time. The Christmas cycle commemorates the incarnation of Christ and anticipates his coming again. The Easter cycle commemorates Christ's death and resurrection.

The church year begins with the season of Advent, which is part of the Christmas cycle. Advent begins four Sundays before Christmas, which in Western churches is celebrated on December 25. The four Sundays of Advent are devoted to remembrance and celebration of Christ's coming at Christmas and to anticipation and preparation for Christ's coming again. The festival of Christmas, perhaps the best known of Christian holidays, celebrates the incar-nation and birth of Christ. In early January, Christians celebrate Epiphany, the disclosure of Christ's divinity to the Gentiles. This holiday focuses on an account found in the Gospel of Matthew of wise men from the East who had followed a star to the birthplace of Christ. They had followed the star from its rising, believing that it signified the birth of a new king, and so they came bearing gifts fitting for a sovereign ruler.

The Sunday following Epiphany celebrates the baptism of Jesus and marks the beginning of ordinary time. This period of ordinary time continues for four to nine Sundays and concludes with a celebration of the transfiguration, an event in which Jesus appears to his disciples with Moses and Elijah and is displayed in his glory. Both in Jesus' baptism and his transfiguration, the voice of God is heard declaring that Christ is the Son of God in whom God is well pleased. The Sundays in this period from Christmas to transfiguration, then, are often spent reflecting on the life of Christ, remembering his teaching and healing ministry.

Following this period of four to nine Sundays of ordinary time, the Easter cycle begins with the season of Lent. The celebration of Easter varies from year to year, which is why the period of ordinary time between Epiphany and Lent varies in length. Easter is celebrated on the first Sunday following the first full moon after the spring equinox on March 21. Eastern and Western churches use slightly different calendars for calculating the date of Easter, so it is not always celebrated on the same Sunday in Eastern Orthodox churches as it is in Roman Catholic and Protestant churches.

The season of Lent consists of the forty days before Easter. Since Lent is a season of penitence as the church remembers and reflects on the death of Christ, Western churches do not count Sundays—the day of the resurrection—as part of Lent. Eastern churches do count Sundays, so the season begins on different days in the two traditions. There are always six Sundays in Lent, but in the West Lent begins on the seventh Wednesday before Easter, Ash Wednesday, and in the East, it begins on the seventh Monday before Easter, Clean Monday. Traditionally the season of Lent has been a season of fasting and sacrifice. Many Christians still refrain from consuming meat during Lent. Others refrain from other favorite foods or activities or undertake special devotional exercises during this time. On Ash Wednesday many churches invite their members into the discipline of Lent by holding services of repentance and the imposition of ashes.

The last Sunday of Lent marks the beginning of Holy Week. This Sunday is called Palm or Passion Sunday. On Palm Sunday Christians remember how Christ entered Jerusalem to the cheers of crowds, the same crowds that called for his death just days later. The crowds greeted Jesus as he entered the city by laying palm fronds on the road as he passed. In many churches the palms that are used during the Palm Sunday service are saved until the following year when they are burned to produce ashes for use during the Ash Wednesday service.

The last three days of Holy Week are of special significance for Christians. On Thursday, which is called Maundy Thursday, the church remembers the night on which Christ was betrayed by his disciple Judas. This was the night on which he instituted the sacrament of communion and also washed his disciples' feet. Many churches hold services of foot washing and communion on Maundy Thursday. Many churches use colored paraments and vestments to indicate which season or festival is being celebrated. Purple is used for Advent and Lent; red, for Pentecost and sometimes Palm/Passion Sunday; green, for ordinary time; and white, for Christmas and Easter. But there is no color for Good Friday and Holy Saturday since the church is stripped bare at the end of Maundy Thursday. Some pastors wear black vestments during these two days. On Friday, which is called Good Friday, the church remembers Christ's death on the cross. Services on Good Friday often include reflections on his last seven words from the cross. On Holy Saturday, the Jewish Sabbath, the church remembers how Christ rested in the tomb.

Lent ends at sunrise on Easter Sunday, when Christians celebrate the resurrection. The season of Easter continues for fifty days, including seven Sundays. On the fortieth day of Easter Christians celebrate the ascension of Jesus into heaven. This is the day on which the resurrected Christ left his disciples, promising to send them the Holy Spirit, and ascended bodily into heaven. On this day Christians affirm the universal lordship of Christ over all things. The season of Easter ends on the seventh Sunday, the day of Pentecost. On this day, Christians remember and celebrate the coming of the Holy Spirit and the establishment of the church.

A period of ordinary time follows Pentecost and continues until the beginning of Advent. Some churches celebrate Trinity Sunday, Christ the King Sunday, and All Saints Day. Others set aside certain days during the year for the commemoration of certain saints.

*Islam.*    There are two main holidays during the Muslim year, and both are tied to special months in the Islamic calendar. The first is the *'id al-fitr* ("the feast of fast-breaking"), which begins with the end of Ramadan and occurs during the first three days of Shawwal, the tenth month. The feast provides an opportunity to celebrate the many blessings received during the preceding month of fasting and self-denial.

It begins with every Muslim family donating food and other goods to the poor to ensure that they, too, will be able to celebrate the conclusion of Ramadan. On the first day of the new month people gather at large mosques and certain outdoor areas to attend a communal prayer gathering. The service begins with a sermon that typically reminds the congregation of the many benefits they obtained during Ramadan, followed by special prayers that are used only during the *'id al-fitr*.

This leads to three days of celebration during which families make the rounds by visiting the homes of relatives and friends, where special meals are prepared in a festive mood. It is also a time to exchange gifts; children, in particular, receive treats and money during these visits. If the feast occurs during a time of year when the weather is nice, many families take trips to local gardens and parks, or destinations farther away, to enjoy each other's company and socialize. After the feast, life slowly returns to the pace it had prior to Ramadan. In most Islamic countries *'id al-fitr* is a national holiday during which businesses are closed and government operations cease.

The most important celebration in the Muslim calendar is the *'id al-adha*, or "the feast of sacrifice." This feast is associated with the final major ritual of the pilgrimage, when, on the tenth day of the month, the pilgrims sacrifice sheep in an act that recalls Abraham's near sacrifice of his son. Qur'an 37:100–12 contains a version of this episode from Abraham's life that is found in Genesis 22 in the Bible. At God's command, Abraham almost kills his son, who remains unnamed in the text, but is prevented from doing so at the last minute. God provides a sheep that Abraham then slaughters and offers to God in place of his son. Muslims have debated the identity of the son throughout history, but most believe it was Ishmael rather than Isaac, who plays the role in Genesis.

On that tenth day of the month of pilgrimage, as the pilgrims are sacrificing their sheep, Muslims throughout the world are doing the same thing as part of the four-day celebration known as *'id al-adha*. As with the *'id al-fitr*, the celebration commences at the mosque, where a sermon is preached and special prayers are said for the occasion. Muslims then return to their homes to prepare the sheep for slaughter. The animal is killed with one swift thrust of a knife over the vein in the neck while the person performing the act says, "In the name of God, the merciful one, the compassionate one." The blood is then drained from the carcass before the animal is butchered and cooked. The act of sacrifice is a highly symbolic one that is meant to commemorate and reenact Abraham's faithfulness to God as he submitted himself to the divine will. The Muslim community expresses that same commitment by mirroring Abraham's act.

Concern for those less fortunate than oneself is a central part of *'id al-adha* as it is for *'id al-fitr*. Families that can afford to buy a sheep to slaughter are expected to consume about one-third of the meat themselves. Another one-third is for their relatives and friends, and they should give the final one-third to the poor and needy. Therefore, the feast does not simply focus on the individual's relationship with God but is a clear reminder about the obligations one has to the wider Muslim community.

A number of other important Islamic celebrations have already been mentioned in prior chapters. The commemoration of the beginning of the revelations to the Prophet Muhammad takes place during the last few days of Ramadan, but that is soon overshadowed by the beginning of 'id al-fitr at the end of the month. Muhammad's birthday, which is observed on the twelfth day of the third month, is an event that is recalled in some Islamic countries, but celebration of it is frowned upon in other places. Among Shia Muslims, the beginning of the first Islamic month is a period of great solemnity. On the tenth day of Muharram in the year 680 Ali's son Husayn was killed by enemy forces at Karbala, and every year his followers reenact that tragedy in a passion play known as a ta'ziya, or consolation.

Chapter Seven

# Relationships

## 1. What does the religion teach about how members of the community should treat one another?

*Judaism.*  *Mitzvah* is the word Judaism invokes to describe an act of ethical distinction. Any act of kindness or support for a deserving cause, for example, is called a mitzvah. The Talmud teaches that it is even a mitzvah to keep one's body clean, to reconcile those who quarrel, to feed animals before one's self, to visit the sick, to bury the dead, and to comfort the mourners. Whatever dignifies or enhances life is a mitzvah.

The performance of mitzvoth (plural) is also the basis for righteous conduct between one person and all others. Whatever spark of divinity one person possesses, all people possess. It cannot be withheld or withdrawn from anyone. It exists equally in people of all races, colors, creeds, and faiths. Economic class or social status is irrelevant in addressing the divine endowment of every human person. If there is one God, there can be only one humanity. The biblical passage that best contains the meaning of mitzvah is the imperative of Leviticus 19:18: "You shall love your neighbor as yourself."

In its practical application the performance of mitzvoth forbids the use of any individual as an instrument in the service of any other. The Torah teaches (Lev. 19:14), "You shall not revile the deaf nor put a stumbling block before the blind." Rabbinic tradition adds that one is not permitted to injure others in any manner, or to oppress, exploit, or humiliate them.

Consequently, one may not deceive others or even withhold the truth from them, since, as the sages explained, words may cut and kill just as savagely as any sword of steel. The rabbinic sage Hillel defined that distinction clearly when he noted, "Do not do unto others what you would not have them do unto you."

Righteous living in terms of mitzvah is more than just a matter of abstaining from evil. It requires active protest and performance in defiance of evil. The rabbis taught that:

> Whoever can protest and prevent his household from committing a sin and does not, is accountable for the sins of his household; if he could protest and prevent his fellow citizens (and does not), he is accountable for the sins of his fellow-citizens; if the whole world, he is accountable for the whole world. (Shabbat 54b)

One of the axioms of rabbinic ethics is that a society which does not allow protest is doomed. One source (Seder Eliahu Rabbah 8) contends that the Egyptians drowned in the Red Sea because they blindly followed Pharaoh's unjust decrees, while another (Shabbat 199b) concludes that Jerusalem fell to the Romans because her people failed to rebuke each other.

The performance of ethical mitzvoth, however, does not demand inordinate courage or uncommon heroics. Righteous conduct is much more a matter of the constant, continuous practice of good deeds. It is a timeless prescription for a healthy society. One such principle is *tzedakah*. This Hebrew term is best defined not as "charity" but, in faithfulness to its authentic root, as "justice" or "righteousness."

Giving to those in need or to urgent causes is not for Judaism simply a matter of love or compassion. *Tzedakah* is an obligation required by law as something that is right, not just kind or thoughtful. As early as the time of the Mishnah, Jewish communities organized systems of progressive taxation to meet the needs of their indigent neighbors. The Mishnah instructs every person to leave unharvested at least a sixtieth of his field; how far one's obligation might exceed the minimum depended on the size of the field and the extent of poverty among the people.

The highest form of *tzedakah* was a concerted effort to restore to the poor the dignity of their own independence. Moses Maimonides, the foremost medieval Jewish authority, declared that:

> [The highest level of charity] is to anticipate charity by preventing poverty; namely, to assist the reduced fellow man, either by a considerable gift or a loan of money, or by teaching him a trade, or by putting him in the way of business, so that he may earn an honest livelihood, and not be forced to the dreadful alternative of holding out his hand for charity.[1]

Even as the donor was expected to contribute his best, so too was the recipient subject to the same obligation. Moral integrity in Judaism required a poor person to accept any kind of job, however menial, in preference to any charitable gift. According to Talmudic law, the community was not required to

---

1. See *Yad HaHazakah, H. Tzedakah 10*, as translated in *Union Prayer Book 2* (Cincinnati: Central Conference of American Rabbis, 1949), 118.

support one who was able but who refused to work. In the Middle Ages, justice yielded to compassion and pity in gradually evolving the legendary figure of the professional schnorrer, a kind of lovable beggar.

Whatever the mitzvah of moral obligation might entail, the property rights of any individual never superseded basic human needs. Jewish law endorsed the principle of private ownership and guarded the rights of an individual to manage his own property. Nonetheless, ownership was ultimately construed in terms of stewardship. Wherever people lived, they were basically tenants subject to God who alone was literally the ultimate land-Lord.

*Christianity.* Christianity does not make a strong distinction between how Christians ought to treat members of the Christian community and how they ought to treat those of other faith traditions. Jesus said, "'In everything do to others as you would have them do to you" (Matt. 7:12). Christians are required not merely to refrain from harming others in ways that they would not want to be harmed but also to seek out the good of others, to "do" for others what they would want done for themselves. This "golden rule" governs how Christians think about their obligations toward others. But the specificity of those obligations is discovered only through a deliberate process of personal and communal discernment. At least three sources inform the process through which Christians discern their obligations toward others.

First, Scripture provides guidance in how Christians ought to treat others. Although the Bible does contain some specific prescriptions and proscriptions, Christians do not, on the whole, understand the Bible to be a rule book designating precisely what one ought to do and refrain from doing. Many of the specific obligations outlined in Scripture are bound to the ancient contexts in which the writings of the Bible were produced. Scripture regarding the permissibility of slaveholding, rules of inheritance, and obligations toward monarchs, for instance, all presuppose circumstances far different from modern, democratic society. As a result, the moral authority of the Bible must always be translated for different times and places.

Instead of seeking specific rules for behavior in the Bible, then, Christians seek to be faithful to the overarching moral themes found in Scripture. Christians look, for example, to the life of Jesus as the preeminent example of moral perfection and self-sacrificial love. They strive to respond to particular moral dilemmas in their own time in a way consonant with the example set by Christ. Christians also look to the moral law of the Old Testament, and to the Ten Commandments, in particular, for an outline of moral obligations toward God and other people. The laws found within the Bible provide a framework for understanding particular moral obligations. The rule to obey one's parents provides broad guidance about the relationships between children and parents without specifying precisely what that obedience will look like in every circumstance. The proscription on adultery sets boundaries on sexual intimacy and provides stability in marriage without specifying precise roles and obligations for spouses. Beyond these rules, moreover, one finds persistent biblical themes reinforcing the need for economic justice, for the wealthy and powerful to care for the poor and dispossessed, for honesty and integrity, and for respect for persons. When Christians look to the example of the early church as it is described in the New Testament for moral guidance, they find that it reinforces these persistent themes of the Old Testament. The early church, for example, distinguished itself from its Greco-Roman culture by providing a network of care and welfare for the widows and poor. Christian churches still emphasize the need for charitable giving to support ministries for the poor. Many churches provide food pantries for the poor and homeless, support shelters for battered women, and send humanitarian aid to regions plagued by famine and natural disasters. Beyond these measures undertaken by particular churches, many Christians advocate for social policies in the political sphere that grow out of their Christian convictions.

Second, the tradition also provides guidance about how Christians should behave toward others. How Christians have framed and responded to moral questions throughout history exercises important influence on how contemporary Christians understand their obligations. The theologian Augustine, for example, struggled with the question of when Christians could endorse the use of military force. His theory of the justifiable use of military force continues to shape Christian thinking on this matter. In addition to guidance on specific moral questions, Christians look to the tradition for a model of moral discernment. The Christian tradition of moral argumentation balances a high value placed on the wisdom of the community with respect for individual conscience. Modern Christians value the tradition as a source of wisdom regarding the obligations they have toward others, but they are also wary of some deeply entrenched biases of the tradition that have sometimes led Christians to endorse slavery, the subordination of women, anti-Semitism, and exploitation of the natural environment.

Natural law constitutes a third source of moral authority. Natural law does not mean something like "the law of nature" but is instead an ethic rooted in the normative experience of humanity; that is, Christians affirm that God has implanted within each person a natural sense of good and evil, a natural sense of obligation. Having this awareness of good and evil is understood to be part of what it means to be made in the image of God. Natural law, then, means the law of human nature—human nature as God created it, that is, not as it is distorted in sin.

*Islam.* It has already been noted that Muhammad's message challenged and transformed the prevailing notions of group identity and allegiance among the people of Arabia. Prior to the rise of Islam, in the period Muslims refer to as *jahiliyyah* ("the time of ignorance"), the tribe was the primary source of support and protection for a person. Islam replaced that tribal-centered system with one in which the Muslim community, or *ummah*, became the group with which people most closely identified themselves. This led to a strong sense of unity among Muslims that continues into the present day. To be a Muslim is to be a member of a worldwide community that creates bonds among all those affiliated with the group.

The foundations of the Islamic ethical system are the Qur'an and the hadith, which provide guidance for social interaction and behavior. Despite the complexity and diversity that exist throughout the Islamic world, Muslims take to heart the Prophet Muhammad's statement recorded in a hadith that "my community is one community." They therefore view each other as equals, and this understanding is the basis for how Muslims are to treat one another.

The heart of Muslim morality is summed up in Qur'an 3:110, which describes the *ummah* in glowing terms: "You are the best community ever brought forth among people. You command what is good, you forbid what is evil, and you worship Allah." As in all religions, Muslim theologians and philosophers throughout history have debated long and hard over the details regarding how members of their faith should behave toward one another. Countless treatises and books have been written that address every aspect of Islamic ethics. In the final analysis, however, it all boils down to the Qur'an passage cited above—Muslims are to do good and refrain from evil. In their day-to-day encounters and interactions with one another, all actions should be guided by that principle.

The communal focus of Islam can be seen in some of the things we have already considered, especially Muslim efforts to assist the poor and needy. The fact that almsgiving is one of the five pillars of the faith that are required of all Muslims is a clear indication that obligations to others are taken seriously. The food that is given to the poor during the two great feasts of the year so that they can celebrate with the rest of the community conveys the same message. These and many similar good works Muslims perform suggest that there is a strong sense of compassion within Islam and that Muslims care deeply for each other.

As essential as membership in the worldwide *ummah* is to Islamic identity, it is primarily in the local arena that one's commitment to fellow Muslims is lived out and expressed. No other context is more important in this regard than the family, which is the primary social institution in Islam. In many Islamic societies family life follows a more or less traditional model in which the husband has the primary economic responsibility and the wife has authority over domestic matters. The Qur'an (17:23) advises children to treat their parents kindly, especially when they attain old age, and parents are expected to provide for and care for their children.

The term *family* often has a very different connotation for Muslims than it does for non-Muslims, especially those living in the West. In many Islamic countries members of the extended family—comprising grandparents, uncles, aunts, and cousins—are a very significant and visible part of a person's life. This means there is a complex web of relationships that must be cultivated and negotiated on a regular, often daily, basis. It is within this context that Islam is lived out, and within it children are first exposed to the morality and ethics of their religion.

Islamic law has played a key role in the development of guidelines for Muslim social interaction. Within the first few centuries of the Muslim era four main schools of Sunni law were established, in addition to the legal system of Shia Islam. These schools are found throughout the world, and Muslims are free to consult authorities within any of them for rulings and legal advice. The four schools all appeal to the same four sources to formulate law: the Qur'an, hadith, consensus, and analogy. While they are usually not profound, differences exist among the schools due to the varying ways they make use of the sources.

Islamic law, or shari'ah, is the law of the land in only a small number of Muslim countries in the present day. In most places, it is used only to decide family-related matters like marriage, divorce, and inheritance. This means that certain punishments mentioned in the Qur'an, like the amputation of one's hand for stealing or the stoning of adulterers, are rarely enforced. Even though most Muslims do not live in a society that is strictly governed by Islam, the ethos and morality that emerge from the Qur'an and other Islamic sources exert a great deal of influence over how they conduct their lives and relate to one another.

## 2. What does the religion teach about how men and women should relate to each other?

*Judaism.*   In the ancient world, with only few exceptions, the political, social, and religious leaders were men. Men enjoyed numerous legal and religious rights denied to women and a distinctly superior social status compared to women.

In ancient Israel, however, the position of women was notably superior to that of their peers in other cultures. In rabbinic law, for example, laws of marital infidelity make no distinction between husband and wife. A woman was permitted to dissolve a marriage if it took place under false pretenses; if the husband was immoral; if his profession was intolerable to her; if they were sexually incompatible; if his demands blemished her reputation; or if he embarrassed her, denied her entry to their home, angered easily, insulted her, beat her, or left her for an unreasonable length of time.

There were no double standards of chastity among Jews, as were common to the rest of the ancient world. The frequent biblical references to love and friendship in the marriages of Israel's patriarchs and matriarchs are a far cry from the chattel relationship between man and wife among other desert peoples, and even in many instances among Greeks and Romans as well.

Outstanding qualities of leadership and wisdom were not infrequently attributed to Jewish women in antiquity. The judgment of Deborah was widely celebrated; Miriam, the sister of Moses, was prominent in any selection of biblical leaders. The Talmud later recounts with admiration the wisdom and scholarship of several unusual women. One of the most remarkable was Beruriah, the wife of Rabbi Meir, whose insights into Jewish law sometimes outshone those of her famous husband.

Some Jewish women achieved fame as lecturers in medieval Europe in an age when the general community treated women as little better than serfs. Dulcie, the daughter of the eminent Rabbi Eleazer of Worms, in addition to supporting her family, was noted for her brilliant Sabbath discourses on Jewish law. Several other women of the fifteenth century were equally acclaimed as outstanding teachers and interpreters of the law. In addition, as wives and mothers Jewish women have always enjoyed a position of such reverence and esteem that their implicit power often surpassed that of any male influence in the family.

In older Jewish communities, the training of children up to the age of six was vested in the mother's hands. Consequently, the person most responsible for teaching them lasting values during their most impressionable years was the woman of the home. Even more crucial was her role as counselor to the entire family. The Talmud taught, "No matter how short your wife is, lean down and take her advice." The sages reinforced that message by adding, "How can a man be assured of having a blessed home? By respecting his wife."

The rabbis tell of a pious couple who, because they could have no children, decided to go their separate ways. Each remarried, and both selected wicked mates. In the end the pious man was corrupted by his evil wife, but the wicked man was redeemed by his pious spouse. The moral of the story, the rabbis taught, is that "it all depends on the wife."

A major consideration is that women were so fully occupied with their domestic duties, it was impossible for them to become deeply involved in the social and religious affairs of the community. Jewish law, for example, stipulates that women are exempt from any rituals that must be performed at a specific time, since their responsibilities to crying or hungry children or other family priorities preclude their participation.

In the Western world, the social and communal role of Jewish women slowly rose to increasingly greater equality, along with that of their non-Jewish neighbors. In religious affairs, however, the changes have not been as universal. Today, in certain Orthodox circles, women are still not permitted to initiate divorce proceedings or to be counted in a minyan, the quorum of ten Jews required for all religious worship. In liberal circles, the status of men and women are virtually equivalent. Women are now ordained as rabbis and cantors, and their numbers are continually increasing. Both Reform and Conservative synagogues have extended religious honors and recognition to men and women equally. In Reform practice there is no longer even an insistence on an exclusively male minyan for worship.

*Christianity.*   The first book of the Bible, Genesis, contains two accounts of creation that provide the theological basis for equality between men and women. The first creation account, found in chapter 1, teaches that men and women were created in the image of God. After everything else had been created, God "created humankind in his image, in the image of God he created them; male and female he created them" (Gen. 1:27). A second account of creation, found in chapter 2, clarifies that the relationship between men and women is to be one of companionship. In this account, God creates the man, Adam, first. In all of creation, no suitable companion can be found for Adam, and so God causes the man to fall into a deep sleep, removes one of his ribs, and creates a woman from it. Adam rejoices to meet his new partner, saying, "this at last is bone of my bones and flesh of my flesh; this one shall be called Woman, for out of Man this one was taken'" (Gen. 2:23).

Eve, the woman, is called Adam's helper, but this term does not in itself signify any kind of subordination since the same term is sometimes applied to God. This vision of an original equality and partnership between men and women is understood to have been shattered by human sinfulness. God declares that because of sin the man will rule over the woman. This declaration is not a description of how God intends men and women to relate to one another; it is a description of how that relationship has in fact become distorted because of sin. Nevertheless, some Christians have come to believe that women ought to be subordinate to men.

The confusion in Christian communities about the status of women is due in part to ambiguity within the Bible itself. On the one hand, the Bible was produced within an ancient, patriarchal culture, and many elements of that culture find expression in the text. On the other hand, one often finds stories in the Bible that place women in positions of leadership that upset cultural expectations. For example, in his epistle to the Galatians, the apostle Paul writes that "in Christ Jesus you are all children of God through faith. As many of you as were baptized into Christ have clothed yourselves with Christ. There is no longer Jew or Greek, there is no longer slave or free, there is no longer male or female; for all of you are one in Christ Jesus" (Gal. 3:26–28). This baptismal formula was often pronounced over new members of the church, signifying that as one enters the Christian community old markers that differentiate status are discarded and new life in Christ begins. Accordingly, one finds accounts of women like Junia and Priscilla, who are leaders in the early church; yet one also finds Pauline proscriptions on women speaking and teaching (1 Cor. 14; 1 Tim. 2:9–15). Early Christianity also offered women a radical new option. They were free to remain unmarried; their status within the Christian community did not depend on their relationship to a man through marriage.

Historically, Christianity has sometimes succumbed to cultural pressures to reinforce patriarchy and has, at other times, offered a liberating vision of equality for men and women. In the modern period, many Christian churches have become intentional and systematic about proclaiming the equality of men and women and affirming the gifts of women for ministry and leadership in the church. Nevertheless, the role of women remains a disputed issue among Christians.

*Islam.* One of the most controversial aspects of Islam for non-Muslims is its view of relations between men and women. The common perception is that Islam endorses male superiority at the expense of women, who are the victims of oppression and subjugation. The Muslim woman's plight is often represented by a disturbing image: she is nothing but a face—sometimes just a pair of eyes—peering out from a long head covering. The rest of her is covered in a dark, loose-fitting garment that further conceals her identity and personhood.

Although this is the experience of some women in the Muslim world, it does not reflect the reality of the majority of them. In some places, as was the case in Taliban-controlled Afghanistan, women are denied their rights and forced to dress this way. This is a very important issue that Muslims must address and respond to. But it is a mistake for non-Muslims to consider it to be representative of the state of affairs in Islam as a whole. There are many other places, like North Africa and Southeast Asia, where men treat women as their equals.

The Qur'an reflects that ambiguity regarding gender relations. On the one hand, many commentators have noted an egalitarian message that is central to the book. According to this perspective, Islam's sacred text recognizes that equality between the sexes was present from the beginning and is an inherent part of creation. "It is God who created you from a single cell, and from it created its mate, so that he might rely upon her" (7:189). Similarly, Qur'an 4:124 says there is no distinction between men and women, who will be rewarded equally if they act rightly. "Whoever does good works, whether male or female, and is a believer—they will enter heaven." Women also have the right to a dowry upon marriage (4:4), and they can inherit money and property from deceased relatives (4:7).

But other passages seem to promote a more male-centered, patriarchal view of things. For example, the number of witnesses required to testify in a court of law is two men or one man and two women (2:282). Elsewhere, male superiority is understood to be due in part to the divine will. "Men are over women because God has given some more than others and because they spend from their wealth" (4:34). That same verse continues on in a way that appears to allow a man to physically abuse his wife under certain conditions.

What are we to do in the face of such conflicting statements? The key is to keep in mind the context out of which the text emerged. There are passages that clearly privilege the male perspective, and there is no denying the fact that certain verses put women in an inferior position. Such texts reflect the norms and practices of seventh-century Arabia, which was a male-dominated society. Should passages that are intended for that context become relevant or normative for later times and places?

This is where the issue of interpretation becomes critical. How one reads and applies these texts determines whether they are interpreted literally or dismissed as irrelevant for our day and age, as many Jews and Christians understand certain biblical passages. This is a critical issue that the Islamic community needs to address, but there is something that further complicates that task. Islam lacks a centralized authority or hierarchy that can make decisions on important issues and speak on behalf of the *ummah* as a whole. There is no single figure or body that has the authority to determine which parts of the Qur'an should be relied on to inform the community about what Islam teaches on male/female relations. This is why we see such a range of responses to the issue. How the classical Islamic sources are interpreted is one of the most important problems facing Islam today because there is so much at stake in it.

Polygamy, divorce, and women's dress are three aspects of Muslim male/female relations that have often attracted the attention of non-Muslims. Muslim men are permitted to have up to four wives according to the Qur'an (4:4), but in many Islamic countries it is illegal to be married to more than one woman at a time. Even in those places where it is permissible it is not very common. Divorce is allowed in Islam—either the woman or the man can initiate it—but there is a *hadith* in which Muhammad declares that among the things that are allowed divorce is the most abominable in God's eyes. The only thing the Qur'an says about women's clothing is that they should dress modestly (24:31), and a very similar thing is said to men in the preceding verse. Wearing a veil on the head or completely covering the body is not endorsed or mentioned in the text. Such practices are usually due to cultural norms that have nothing to do with religion, or they are supported by interpretations of other passages that do not speak specifically about how women should dress.

## 3. What does the religion teach about people who follow other faiths?

*Judaism.*   In Jewish tradition all people, regardless of race, religion, or ethnic origin, are equally God's children, equally precious as human beings, equally deserving of justice and mercy from any human agency or institution. Differences among individuals are a consequence of their personal performance. No person is inherently better than any other.

Judaism is virtually oblivious to race. Although traditional sources trace the origins of the Jewish people to the patriarchs of Israel, and although biblical evidence exists of early exclusionary practices by Israelites, kinship is never linked entirely to blood descent. Under existing provisions of Jewish practice, any person who chooses to join the Jewish people and to follow the Jewish faith enjoys equal status with every Jew who was born into the covenant. No one is excluded any longer from membership because of racial or ethnic differences. The standards for entry into Judaism are admittedly demanding, but they are entirely a matter of theological, moral, ritual, and educational preparedness.

Although the requirements may be stringent, conversion to Judaism is not a precondition for salvation in this world or the next. One of the Talmudic rabbis stated explicitly, "The righteous of all the world have a share in the world-to-come" (*b Sanhedrin* 13:2). One chooses to become a Jew not for the purpose of achieving eternal rewards, but for the purpose of building a better world. Any decent human being may expect whatever rewards accrue to a life of justice and goodness in this world or the next.

In some ways it is even easier for a non-Jew to achieve lasting reward than it is for a Jew. Eligibility for the world-to-come requires a non-Jew only to follow the seven commandments of the covenant that God consummated with Noah. That covenant embodies for Judaism the fundamental precepts that should govern all civilized society. It includes prohibitions against (1) idolatry, (2) incest and adultery, (3) bloodshed, (4) the profanation of God's name, (5) injustice and lawlessness, (6) robbery, and (7) inhumane conduct, such as cutting a limb from a living animal. In addition, Talmudic literature is filled with legends about heathens who supposedly "acquired the world-to-come" by single acts of extraordinary compassion or courage. By contrast, Jews seeking assurance of eternal life are expected to observe as many of the 613 commandments of the Torah as may apply.

The recognition among Jews that others possess sufficient spiritual merit for divine approval is a unique distinction unparalleled in any Western religious tradition. It helps to explain the approach to conversion among many rabbinic authorities who will accept Jews by choice who are sincere and determined, but will not actively or aggressively seek them. Indeed, Halakkah (Jewish law) instructs a rabbi to discourage potential proselytes and to yield only if they persist in their request.

A more recent development of liberal Jewish attitudes toward non-Jews, especially in a democratic setting, is a recognition that every religious discipline contributes to the totality of spiritual truth. The quality of the whole human enterprise is better and brighter precisely because of the differences among peoples and civilizations. One culture stimulates another and encourages a continuous process of reassessment and renewal. Every religion challenges every other; each contributes some insight or value that the others cannot fully grasp or understand. Unfortunately, the reality of the human condition does not make this proposition easy to apply, but that misfortune does not make it any less true.

For the Jewish people the contribution of Judaism is endowed with a special distinction of its own. The dictates of reason are an essential component in its formulation of faith. Its ethical idealism is imperishable but practical. Social justice is the heart of its message. Physical and spiritual reality are blended in a clear but gentle balance. Its legacy of language and literature, ritual pageantry, dedication to freedom of conscience, and reverence for life are all crown jewels of the human spirit.

At the same time, most liberal Jews will not pretend that Judaism has exhausted every measure of truth and goodness in the universe. Some have developed better insights into mysticism, others have concentrated more intently on the quest for peace, while still others have created more dramatic and inspiring rituals. Most religious faiths, therefore, do not compete with one another but complement one another. Most possess their own share of truth and merit and have a right to thrive and flourish. Out of its own unique contribution, every major faith ensures that the world is far better served with a multiplicity of beliefs than it could be out of rigid uniformity. Indeed, diversity is the prerequisite for all creativity. The world could not endure without it.

*Christianity.* Christians affirm that people of other faiths are the beloved creatures of God, made in the image of God. Christian theology, moreover, affirms that God is revealed to all people through nature and reason. This universal human knowledge of God is known as general revelation, and it accounts for why people worldwide practice religion and pray to God or to gods. Nature points toward its creator, though human beings may misunderstand or misinterpret it and find themselves worshiping idols and false gods rather than the true God. In spite of this propensity to misinterpret nature and to use our reason imperfectly, all people may come to know that God exists and is good. Beyond this general knowledge of God's existence and goodness, Christians also affirm that God is known by all to be just. God has implanted within all people a sense of morality, a "natural law" that guides them in right behavior and forms the foundation of a universal human ethic. For this reason, even those who have no knowledge of the Christian faith know, for example, that murder is wrong, that parents should care for their children, and that the powerful should protect the defenseless.

General revelation ensures that God is known as creator and that the justice God requires is known to all. But Christians believe that general revelation does not provide knowledge sufficient for salvation. From nature and the use of reason one could not know that Jesus Christ is God incarnate who lived, died, and rose for human salvation. This knowledge comes through what is known as special revelation, the way in which God is revealed for salvation especially through the history of Israel, in the life of Christ, and in Scripture as it witnesses to these events. Because these truths must be learned from the witness of Scripture or from Christian believers, Christians place a high value on evangelism and missionary activity to spread word of the gospel with the hope that members of other religious traditions will hear and believe the good news of salvation.

Christians regard the Jewish faith differently from other faith traditions. Christianity regards itself as the natural continuation of the faith of the children of Israel. The God of the Old Testament is the only true God. The promises God made to the children of Israel are fulfilled in Jesus Christ. In this sense, Christians regard their faith as having superseded Judaism. This supercessionism can lead Christians to adopt an arrogant attitude toward Jews, whom they regard as stubbornly refusing to recognize that Christianity is the true meaning of the Jewish faith. Other Christians, however, have acknowledged that God's faithfulness to all generations means that God will keep all of the promises made to the Jewish people regardless of whether they come to faith in Christ. Especially after the Holocaust, many Christians have called into question the supercessionist view of the relationship between Christianity and Judaism. Christians also acknowledge a special relationship with Islam because Muslims worship the same God as Jews and Christians, but Christians differ with both Jews and Muslims in their interpretation of who Jesus is.

Christians believe that salvation comes only through Christ. Yet some Christians also affirm that God may redeem people of other faiths even if they do not convert to Christianity. There are at least three different ways in which Christians have thought about the salvation of non-Christians. The first position, known as exclusivism, is probably best known and most widely believed. The exclusivist position holds that salvation is exclusively for those who explicitly confess Jesus Christ as savior. The Gospel of John says that "God so loved the world that he gave his only Son, so that everyone who believes in him may not perish but have eternal life" (3:16). According to the exclusivist position, this means that people of other faiths cannot be redeemed unless they come to believe in Christ and convert to Christianity. Exclusivists do not necessarily believe that all non-Christians are consigned to everlasting suffering in hell; there is an alternate way of thinking about what it means to "perish." Some have articulated a view known as annihilationism, the view that God simply unmakes those who are not redeemed. They understand hell to mean life apart from God, and since life is only possible in God, those who do not come to God through Christ are annihilated; they cease to exist and, therefore, experience neither the joy of everlasting life in God nor suffering of any kind.

Karl Rahner, a twentieth-century Roman Catholic theologian, articulated a second way of thinking about the salvation of non-Christians. His position has been described as inclusivism. Rahner argued that salvation comes only through Christ, but that those of other faith traditions may be redeemed in Christ without being aware that Christ is the agent of their redemption. Christ may work redemptively in other religions so that people who practice those religions faithfully may objectively encounter Christ without being subjectively aware of it. He called the redeemed of other faith traditions "anonymous Christians." Nevertheless, Rahner insisted that anyone who has an "existentially real" encounter with the Christian faith cannot be redeemed outside of it. In other words, once a person becomes subjectively aware of Christ as the agent of redemption, no religion other than Christianity can convey saving grace. In this way Rahner made room for the possibility that God redeems those who have never had the opportunity to hear the gospel.

Universalism constitutes a third way in which Christians have thought about the possibility of salvation for non-Christians. Universalism means simply that God redeems all people. Universalists point to passages of Scripture such as 1 Corinthians 15:21–22, which says that "since death came through a human being, the resurrection of the dead has also come through a human being; for as all die in Adam, so all will be made alive in Christ." Some universalists would insist that God is ultimately sovereign over all creation, and that the nature of God is loving and gracious so that ultimately no aspect of creation will escape God's sovereign grace. Others would leave open the possibility that everyone is redeemed, without positively affirming it, because they wish to respect God's freedom to act in whatever way God sees fit and to redeem whomever God pleases. Finally, many Christians simply leave the question of the salvation of non-Christians to the mystery of the divine will, trusting that God will always be both merciful and just.

*Islam.* Judaism, Christianity, and Islam are called the Abrahamic religions because they all trace their origins back to the patriarch Abraham. Islam calls attention to that common family ancestry and acknowledges the connections that exist among the three faiths. Qur'an 3:84 recounts what Muhammad is told to teach his followers about the prophets who came before him: "We believe in God, what has been revealed to us, what was revealed to Abraham, Ishmael, Isaac, Jacob, and the tribes, and what was given to Moses, Jesus and the prophets from their Lord. We do not make a distinction among any of them, and to God we submit." Muslims are required to respect all of the prophets equally and to consider each one a legitimate recipient of God's revelation.

Islam acknowledges the validity of the other two monotheistic religions, but it also maintains they suffer from some shortcomings. According to the Muslim understanding of revelation, the followers of the prior prophets distorted the message and did not record it in the form in which it was given to them. In other words, the Bible does not accurately relate the content of the revelation received by Moses, Jesus, and the other prophets. This necessitated the sending of a final prophet—Muhammad—whose people preserved the message intact in the Qur'an. He is called the "seal of the prophets" (33:40) because the prophetic line comes to an end with him.

Islam's relationship with Judaism and Christianity is therefore a complicated and ambiguous one. It considers them to be corecipients of God's word through the prophets, yet it maintains that only it has perfectly communicated that word to the world. Like Jews and Christians, Muslims believe they have a special covenant with God. They claim their faith supersedes the earlier religions in a way similar to how some Christians view Christianity's relationship with Judaism. In short, with the coming of Islam the other monotheistic faiths were rendered obsolete and unnecessary. This partly explains the important role that outreach, or *da'wa*, has in Islam. Because it is the final, corrected version of monotheistic faith it invites all people to join the *ummah*.

Despite that missionary dimension, Islam does not force itself on non-Muslims. There is a longstanding tradition of tolerance in Islam that is best summed up in Qur'an 2:256: "There is no compulsion in religion." People can be encouraged to embrace the faith, but conversion to Islam is ultimately something that is left up to God alone. A person cannot be compelled to convert. This spirit of tolerance and coexistence goes back to the time of the Prophet Muhammad, whose "Constitution of Medina" established guidelines for how Muslims, Jews, Christians, and other non-Muslims would live together in that city. It is also seen in the term "people of the book," a designation found in the Qur'an that is used for Jews and Christians. This title underscores the high regard Muslims have for their fellow monotheists, who have also been privileged recipients of divine revelation.

The theological disagreements Islam has with Christianity are more profound than those it has with Judaism. The main reason for this is the Christian belief that Jesus is God in human form. From the Muslim perspective, this is an example of *shirk*—associating something from creation with the uncreated nature of God—the only sin God will not forgive. The Qur'an points out the error in this thinking a number of times: "They have disbelieved who say, 'Truly, God is the Messiah, the son of Mary'" (5:17). In one passage (5:116) Jesus denies he is divine and tells God his followers are misguided. The Islamic text also dismisses belief in the trinity as another example of *shirk* that demonstrates Christianity has distorted God's intended message (5:73). Christians often find such texts disturbing or insulting because they call into question central beliefs of their faith.

At the same time, Jesus is a very prominent and important figure in the

Qur'an and for Muslims. He is a prophet who is virginally conceived, performs miracles, and is given special titles like "messiah" and "word from God." His mother Mary is the only woman mentioned by name in the Qur'an, and chapter 19 of the book is named after her. Jesus is highly respected by Muslims, but they and Christians will never be able to agree on the question of his identity. The best that can be hoped for is that they agree to differ in a spirit of mutual respect and tolerance.

Chapter Eight

# Social Issues

## 1. What is the view of the relationship between religion and politics?

*Judaism.* History provides a Jew with ample reason for developing political and social sensitivity to the needs of one's neighbors. The Torah teaches (Exod. 23:9), "You shall not oppress a resident alien; you know the heart of an alien, for you were aliens in the land of Egypt."

Because of their experience with oppression for centuries, Jews were expected to feel compassion for other scapegoats. Roots of social concern run deep in Jewish history and theology. Whatever concept of God a Jew chooses to follow, that belief always includes a moral imperative to do justice. If one believes God cares for all people, then so should we all. If one perceives God as the power within people and nature that explains the social order, then we all are responsible to protect it and defend it. Others may speak of the covenant between God and Israel that binds a Jew to observe the divine mandate for truth and righteousness. One may even propose that the Jewish people have chosen themselves to be messengers of right conduct and to enjoin the rest of the world to emulate their example.

Jews are also especially preoccupied with social issues because of their experience with anti-Semitism. Anti-Semitism increases in proportion to the level of frustration in any society and its insatiable quest for a scapegoat to vent its anger. Jews therefore eagerly strive to achieve a society that affords maximum self-expression for all its members, thereby minimizing frustration and weakening the impulse to inflict harm on helpless minorities. A closed society that suppresses basic civil liberties poses a potential disaster for the most vulnerable segments of any community, which is why Jews generally have always labored for a free and open body politic.

Bernard Malamud summed it up well in *The Fixer* when he noted, "We're all in history, that's sure, but some are more than others, Jews more than some. . . . One thing I've learned . . . there's no such thing as unpolitical man, especially a Jew. . . . You can't sit still and see yourself destroyed."

The roots of political protest among Jews can be traced to the preexilic prophets of Israel who challenged the most cherished beliefs of the people. The Israelites under the reign of Jeroboam II believed that soon "the day of the Lord" would arrive, a day of triumph over all their enemies. Amos shook their complacency by warning that the day of the Lord would be one of darkness and not light, a day of disaster. The people would suffer, because they had turned aside from their covenant of justice.

After the exile, when the priesthood tried to hold the small Judean community together, the concept of a *goy kadosh* ("a holy nation") slowly evolved. Although the priestly period was marked primarily by religious and political conservatism, the idea of a *goy kadosh* resonated with radical implications. The root meaning of *kadosh* is "to be set apart for a higher spiritual purpose." The priests, and later the rabbinic sages, insisted that the Jewish people should maintain their distance from others so that their own ethical standards might not be tainted by the popular immoralities of their time. The biblical and rabbinic ideal called for moral concern for all humankind.

The very purpose of Jewish existence was "to make the right go forth among the nations" and "to be a light unto the nations that [God's] salvation may be known in all the earth" (Isa. 49:6b). The justification for Jewish distinctiveness was that the Jewish people might better fulfill their messianic mission.

One of the most decisive justifications for political activism in Jewish terms is the lesson of the Hasidic story that tells of the *tzadik* (a wholly righteous person) who was going to Sodom and Gemorrah to rebuke the people for their evil deeds. A passerby mocked him: "You know that no one will pay you any heed. You can never change the way they are." To which the *tzadik* replied, "I know I can never change the way they are, but by speaking out, I can keep them from changing the way I am."

On the subject of race relations, the sages taught that God formed Adam of dust from all over the world, so that no race on earth can ever be told, "This soil is not your home."

Jews are thus more likely than others to support policies that would deal more vigorously with the social, educational, and economic conditions that breed poverty, frustration, and violence, as opposed to relying entirely on stricter law and order. Whether the reason be minority status, religious tradition, education, or class (or a combination of all these factors), Jews are still represented out of proportion to their numbers in movements that would secure social justice and preserve our civil liberties.

*Christianity.*   Christian views of the relationship between church and state have evolved over time in response to dramatic changes in the political order. We can identify three such changes. The first occurred when the Emperor Constantine converted to Christianity and the religion changed from being an illegal and persecuted sect to being the official religion of state. The second dramatic shift happened in the West when the collapse of the Roman Empire led to the loss of a strong, centralized government and the emergence of feudalism in its place. The third dramatic change came with the emergence of modern democratic states.

Under the Christianized Roman Empire, Christians tended to operate with a theocratic view of the relationship between church and state. Theocracy means that the law of the state is an expression of the law of God. Eastern Orthodox Christians, for instance, would have insisted that the emperor was the vicar of God on earth, responsible for ordering society according to the divine will. Matters of the political order and matters of spiritual concern were . often fused. In medieval Europe, especially after the collapse of the Roman Empire there, the pope often took on strong political leadership. On Christmas day in the year 800, the pope crowned Charlemagne as Holy Roman Emperor. This act implied that political power flowed from the pope to political authorities. The move also inflamed the rivalry between East and West because there was already a Roman Emperor reigning in the East, and just as there can be only one God, Eastern Christians insisted, so there can only be one emperor, one vicar of God on earth.

By the time of the Protestant Reformation, independent nation-states had begun to develop in Europe, and the possibility of a unified, theocratic empire had long faded. The emerging Protestant movements often depended on the protection of heads of state who wished to establish power independent of the papacy. Luther's reformation in Germany, for instance, depended heavily on the support of the German princes. Luther developed a theory of the relationship between church and state that is often described as the "two kingdoms" model. His model drew heavily on a theory articulated centuries earlier by Augustine, who had argued that God had established "two cities," an earthly city and a heavenly city. The earthly city is the realm of politics and civil concerns. The heavenly city is the true home of Christians, who travel through the earthly city only as pilgrims. The two cities would coexist throughout history until at last God established an everlasting kingdom on earth that vanquished the earthly city. The question of how Christians should relate to the earthly city they travel through as pilgrims remained open to debate. Luther proposed that Christians may inhabit both realms simultaneously. God has provided the political order so that human sinfulness will not be given free reign. The civil order restrains our worst sinful impulses. Christians may participate in the state insofar as advancing its causes does not conflict with their Christian obligations.

Another group, known as the Radical Reformers, shared the two-kingdoms model with Luther but disagreed with his view that Christians may legitimately participate in matters of state. According to the Radical Reformers, Christians are called out of the worldly kingdom and should not participate in its affairs. A citizen of the kingdom of God must renounce citizenship in worldly kingdoms and the conflicting loyalties that go with it. Christians should not swear oaths, serve in the military, or hold political office. Christians should not serve as judges or magistrates or exercise any kind of political power. Christians may attempt to influence the state by serving as witnesses to Christ's call to nonviolence, but they may not become internally enmeshed in its structures and institutions.

John Calvin, a second-generation Protestant Reformer, offered a different way of thinking about the relationship between church and state. Calvin argued that the state existed not simply to restrain evil but also to promote social welfare and righteousness. Accordingly, governments ought to provide not only police and military forces but also agencies that promote health, education, and the arts. He rejected the idea that there are two separate kingdoms and instead insisted that both the church and the state exist to serve God's purposes. In sixteenth-century Geneva this model took on a theocratic form, but later Calvinists have advanced models of the state in which the state exists to serve the good without becoming an arm of the church. According to the Calvinist model, political office is a vocation, a calling. As such, Christians who are called to serve in government posts may do so in order to pursue policies that restrain evil and promote righteousness.

*Islam.*   Muslims believe religion is an essential aspect of a person's identity that influences every part of one's life. Faith is not something someone draws on solely in moments of need or celebrates only on a particular day of the week. Islam is a total way of life that affects how Muslims think and behave whether they are in the mosque, the home, or the marketplace. Every area of human existence comes under the authority of Islam.

Consequently, there is no separation between religion and politics in Islam. The close connection between the two was established in the earliest days of the faith, when the Prophet Muhammad was considered to be both a religious guide and a political leader. When he migrated from Mecca to Medina in 622 to serve as a judge for the people there, Muhammad insisted that the local population acknowledge him as both a mediator who would settle their disputes and a prophet who had been chosen by God. Similarly, members of his own community considered him to be a model of piety who was the supreme authority in matters of faith, as well as a statesman whose political leadership played a key role in shaping the nascent Muslim *ummah*.

This paradigm was adopted by the early successors who assumed the mantle of authority over the Islamic community. The four Rightly Guided Caliphs, who ruled between 632 and 661, also functioned as religious and political leaders who enjoyed special status by virtue of their having been Muhammad's companions. As the Islamic Empire grew, however, the demands and challenges of governing a community that was spread over a vast geographic area led to changes in how leadership was conceived and exercised. Political and religious authority were eventually separated and no longer identified with the same individual. Various religiously based positions and offices—like lawyer, judge, and theologian—emerged, and these individuals became the de facto authorities on issues related to faith. This arrangement has continued into the present day, and there is currently no Islamic country that gives complete religious and political authority to one person.

But that division of labor does not mean there is a separation between the two spheres. Just the opposite is the case. In Islam, religion is supposed to inform and influence the political arena. There is no clear agreement on what the ideal Islamic state should look like, but it is consistently held that Muslim principles and values must be at its core. Some maintain that Islamic law, or *shariah*, must be fully implemented as the law of the land so that all can come under the authority of God and fully submit themselves to the divine will. Others prefer a modified version that would reserve Islamic law for only certain areas of life, like marriage, divorce, and inheritance. Still others believe it is only necessary that the state and its representatives not hold views or engage in activities that go against the teachings and spirit of Islam.

In the present day, Islamic involvement in the political process takes various forms. The Iranian Revolution of 1979 led to the establishment of an Islamic Republic that remains the fullest example of that form of government in the world. The Council of Guardians, comprising a group of religious scholars who are led by the Grand Ayatollah, ensures that all actions of the president and the parliament are in accordance with Islamic law and principles. In other countries, like Saudi Arabia and the Sudan, Islamic law governs most areas of life, and the political process is strongly influenced by religious beliefs and rulings. Elsewhere, as in Tunisia, Morocco, and Malaysia, a more secular model is in place, with a wider separation of religion and politics, not unlike what is found in the West.

An interesting development in recent years is the growing presence of

Islamic groups that seek to operate within the system in order to influence the shape and direction of the government. In many cases, these organizations believe the ruling party is not Islamic enough, and they attempt to rectify that situation. One of the most important of these movements is the Muslim Brotherhood, an Egyptian organization founded in 1928 that various Egyptian leaders have sought to marginalize, and at times outlaw, throughout its history. It is a popular group that has been allowed to operate more openly in recent years, but it is still forbidden to function as an official political party. Nonetheless, in the most recent Egyptian elections a significant number of candidates associated with the Muslim Brotherhood were elected to parliament, which suggests it is becoming a force to be reckoned with in Egyptian politics.

One of the most hotly debated topics today concerns the compatibility between Islam and democracy. It is true that democracy remains an unrealized ideal within the Islamic world, but many observers—Muslim and non-Muslim alike—maintain that this is due to a variety of historical, cultural, and political factors rather than to an inherent opposition to democracy within the religion. Many argue that certain concepts central to Islam—like consultation, consensus, and the use of independent reasoning—can aid in the formation of a distinctly Islamic form of democracy.

## 2. What is the view of the relationship between religion and science?

*Judaism.*   One of the fundamental precepts of Judaism is that everything in the universe is a unified whole, that there are no dichotomies between the physical and the spiritual or between the sacred and the mundane. A corollary of this conviction is that our ethics also flows from this universal harmony; reality will not permit double standards, be they in matters physical or moral. Unity is an essential key to understanding how all existence functions.

Science informs us that the universe is indeed one in ways our ancestors could not even have imagined. Time and space are one; we are told that they are in fact aspects of the same ultimate reality. We have also learned that matter and energy are one. As difficult as it may be for some to understand, one may even speak of matter as energy at rest; energy may simply be matter in motion. Biologists further add that the organic and inorganic are actually one; they no longer think in terms of total separation between animate and inanimate life forms. The potential for life was present even before life itself first appeared; viruses, for example, may well be a transition or bridge between the inorganic and organic.

We now know, as our ancestors could only have hoped, that the same physical laws that operate on a macro scale also apply in the same way on a micro scale. With the benefit of the most powerful radio telescopes, we can now confirm that the chemical elements that make up the components of our own bodies exist as well in the farthermost reaches of outer space. The movement of protons, electrons, and neutrons within the atom corresponds strikingly to the movement of planets in a solar system around the sun.

The arrangement of chromosomes within living cells is precisely the same in number and function in a celery stalk, a toad, or a human being. The evidence is impressive and can be documented repeatedly. The entire universe in its vast complexity is one ultimate basic reality. As Judaism proclaims in the watchword of its faith, the Shema, "Hear, O Israel, the Eternal, our God, the Eternal really is one!"

The blending of modern scientific thought with ancient Jewish teaching has been noted by many competent observers. One such eminent scholar, Dr. Ralph W. Burhoe, has noted,

> The scientific faith that all things are variants in a single system, that one law rules the cosmos from end to end, from the largest to the smallest, is a faith that grows stronger with each succeeding new discovery that shows the relationship between phenomena that previously did not seem to be related. We can be confident now with the knowledge we possess that a clear continuity exists from molecule to amoeba to humanity. Every individual is inextricably linked to every other human being and to every other life form in the universe. We are indeed all brothers.[1]

Judaism can also acknowledge that nature provides us with ethical guidelines for personal behavior. Much of that confidence rests on an appreciation for the teachings of evolution. A study of evolution manifests decisive trends toward organization and order, toward uniqueness and individuality, toward increased freedom and enlarged spirituality. Prior to the appearance of humanity, evolution proceeded automatically in these directions. From the human point forward, however, they are no longer automatic. Further movement in these directions will continue only with human initiative, only if people act in harmony with those patterns. Judaism can apply these modern, scientifically oriented terms to explain its conviction that people are partners in God's creative work.

The Shema is seemingly just a statement of faith, but in the larger context of science and secular knowledge, this pronouncement proclaims an entire

---

1. Cited in H. Shapley, ed., *Science Ponders Religion* (New York: Appleton-Century-Crafts, 1960), 80f.

worldview not just about God but about the universe, humanity, and life itself. In Jewish terms, science and religion are indispensable partners in deciphering the mystery of existence.

*Christianity.*   Throughout the history of Christianity there have been ques tions about the relationship between what can be learned through the use of reason and what is taught in Scripture, and these questions remain largely open. Christians differ significantly in how they understand the relationship between faith and science. Especially with the advent of evolutionary biology Christians have had to rethink what their faith teaches regarding the creation of humankind. Did God create human beings, in their current form, in a special act? Or did humanity arise out of a gradual process that also shaped other species? Contributions from disciplines such as geology and physics, which reveal a very ancient beginning for the earth and the cosmos as a whole, have also caused Christians to revisit their views of how science and faith intersect. Should Genesis 1, with its presentation of a six-day creation, be interpreted literally or does it present theological truths in metaphorical form?

Modern Christians may assume that the tradition interpreted Genesis 1 literally, and that only in recent times have new interpretations been advanced, but such was not always or consistently the case. In his commentary on the book of Genesis, for instance, John Calvin, a sixteenth-century Protestant Reformer, expressed a view common among Christians of his and earlier times that the creation accounts contained in that book should not be mistaken for literal or scientific accounts of how things came to be. Instead, Genesis contains a theological account of the relationship between God and the creation. Calvin chided those who asked of Genesis, whose author he took to be Moses, questions it was not prepared to answer, saying, "For as it became a theologian, he has respect to us rather than to the stars. . . . Moses wrote in a popular style things which, without instruction, all ordinary persons endued with common sense are able to understand; but astronomers investigate with great labor whatever the sagacity of the human mind can comprehend."[2]

Calvin and theologians like him argue that Scripture teaches what is necessary for salvation, reveals the nature of God, and guides believers toward righteousness. Its intent is not to present objective historical, geographical, or scientific facts. These things can be discerned through the use of reason and by observing the natural order. Ultimately, such Christians expect that what is revealed through reason and what is revealed in Scripture will not conflict,

2. John Calvin, "Commentary on Genesis," vol. 1, chap. 1, v. 16. The text is available on the Christian Classics Ethereal Library at http://www.ccel.org/c/calvin/comment3/comm_vol01/htm/vii.htm.

but during the process of discovery, it may remain unclear how these two sources of truth correspond. Some Christian theologians will go so far as to claim that what is discovered through science may properly shape and correct theological claims.[3] Theological claims about the extent of human free will may be qualified by insights from psychology and sociology. Claims about natural evil—evil that is not directly caused by human sinfulness—will be informed by insights from the natural sciences.

In sharp contrast to this tradition of accepting scientific accounts of creation that differ from a literal interpretation of Genesis, some evangelical Christians, especially in America, find faith and science, especially evolutionary biology, to be in irreconcilable conflict. These Christians would argue that Genesis teaches that God created everything in six days, approximately six thousand years ago, and that humankind began with two individuals, Adam and Eve, whom God created at that time. The idea that humanity evolved from other life forms, they would insist, compromises the fundamental theological affirmation that humanity was created in the image of God. They would also argue that science, freed from an atheistic bias, would not conflict with these claims. Evolutionary claims, they argue, are unsupported by the evidence, and careful observation of the natural order indicates that it is too complex and well-ordered to have come into existence without an intelligent designer.

*Islam.*   The Qur'an and the sayings of the Prophet Muhammad tell Muslims to study and learn from the world around them. They are urged to examine their environment so that they can develop an understanding of the created order and their place within it. At the same time, they will come to a deeper appreciation of the power and majesty of the God who brought everything into existence. Muslims understand this to be an invitation to engage in scientific inquiry, experimentation, and analysis.

During the medieval period that eventually gave rise to the Scientific Revolution Islam exerted a tremendous amount of influence on the intellectual heritage of the non-Muslim world. Were it not for the Islamic community it is probable that some of the most prominent figures of antiquity would have disappeared from the pages of history, silently buried in oblivion. The foremost examples of this are the classical Greek philosophers like Plato and Socrates. At an early stage in Islamic history their writings were translated into Arabic by Muslims, who preserved them for centuries as the only extant copies of the works. Later, when Muslims had the opportunity to interact and

---

3. See, for example, James Gustafson, *An Examined Faith: The Grace of Self Doubt* (Minneapolis: Augusburg Fortress Press, 2003).

live with Christians and Jews, they reintroduced into Europe the works of these important thinkers. Muslim contributions in this area went well beyond preservation because they also offered interpretations of the writings of the Greek philosophers that had an impact on how the non-Muslim world came to understand these works.

Muslims were not only engaged in the preservation and interpretation of literary texts but were also responsible for some of the most significant inventions and discoveries in science and related fields. It has already been noted how important Muslim advances in medicine were for European physicians and surgeons, as seen in the fact that Ibn Sina's (Avicenna's) textbook was their standard reference work for centuries. Mathematics is another field that was heavily influenced by Muslim scholars. Algebra, coming from the Arabic word *al-jabr*, was invented by Muslim mathematicians. Algorithms take their name from Al-Khawarizmi (d. 840), who was one of the most brilliant mathematicians the Islamic world produced. Muslims invented the concept of zero, which is a foundation for the numbering system used throughout the world. Euclid's writings on geometry are known to us today only because they were translated into Arabic and preserved by Muslims.

The Islamic world also made important contributions to many other areas of science, including chemistry, botany, pharmacology, and zoology. One field that deserves special mention is astronomy, which Muslims took keen interest in from the earliest days of Islam. Many new stars were discovered by Muslims, who composed numerous astronomical tables as a result of their observations that influenced the development of European astronomy. The world's first truly scientific observatory, at Maraghah in Persia, was built in the heart of the Muslim world. Among the many astronomical tools and instruments invented by Muslims the most well-known is the astrolabe, which allows one to fix the position of the sun and stars in the sky, and assists in determining the precise time of day. Muslim interest in astronomy was often directly related to the practice of their faith since knowledge of the sun's location in the sky and the direction of Mecca would determine when and how they prayed.

Some of the most significant works of translation and discovery took place in Spain, during a period known in Spanish as *Convivencia,* when Muslims, Jews, and Christians lived together and learned from one another. Between the eighth and fifteenth centuries, members of the three faiths coexisted in an environment of tolerance and respect that benefited all. During this time remarkable achievements were made in science, art, literature, and architecture, and the era still stands as a shining example of what is possible when people of different faiths come together in a spirit of trust and cooperation.

The West profited from Muslim advances in science and eventually developed a strong scientific tradition of its own. In recent times the non-Muslim world has generally surpassed the Muslim world in the areas of science and technology, and this situation has been addressed by Muslims in various ways. At one extreme are those who see this as evidence that the people of the West have become too secular, and therefore conclude that Muslims should have nothing to do with them. At the other end are those who maintain that the Muslim world needs to become more like the West and recover its commitment to scientific inquiry.

Despite these differences and debates, Muslims now face a challenge similar to the one confronting Jews and Christians as science continues to expand human knowledge and understanding. Concepts like evolution and advancements like cloning sometimes challenge the assumptions of their sacred texts and the teachings of their communities, and this raises profound questions about the nature of faith and its role in the world.

### 3. What are some of the religion's teachings in the area of human sexuality?

*Judaism.*   Judaism concedes that biologically a human being is part of the animal kingdom. Spiritually, however, it insists that every person is also little lower than the angels. Among the lower animals, the sex drive is a purely biological one, but in the human animal the situation is much more complicated.

While there is little controversy over the belief that sex in modern civilized societies must have more than biological meaning, there are wide differences expressed by various religious groups about the question of sinfulness or the basic evil nature of sex. Rabbinic literature records the observation of Rabbi Samuel ben Nahman, who noted the verse from Genesis "And behold it was very good" and observed, "This alludes to the 'impulse to evil'—the *yetser hara*. Is then the 'impulse to evil' ever good? Yes, for were it not for the 'impulse to evil,' no man would build a house, nor marry a wife, nor beget children, nor engage in trade."

The Talmud identified sex as an aspect of the *yetser hara*—"the impulse to evil." Yet it persisted in calling that impulse "good," not only because it too was a divine creation but because this impulse was part of the drive that makes for progress. It was only in its unleashed and uncontrolled expression that the sexual impulse was considered evil.

Sexuality in Judaism, then, was almost always considered to be a necessary and healthy function of human personality. Sex was not sinful or shameful. It is a blessing to humanity. Indeed, this attitude toward the enjoyment of the pleasures of life—in moderation—is one of the distinguishing features of Judaism.

Although a certain prudishness prevailed periodically in Jewish communities, Jews usually exhibited an exceptionally open and honest approach to sexual morality. While a debate still rages in many places about the wisdom of sex education in public schools, Jewish students of the Talmud covered such topics as puberty, conception, menstruation, birth control, and breast feeding by the time they were eleven or twelve years of age. The subject of sex was not obscene, but a natural function of human behavior.

These students, therefore, were not shocked, as some modern readers might be, to learn that Jewish law provided that husband and wife should not have sexual intercourse while either is intoxicated, sluggish, or in mourning, nor when the wife is asleep, nor if the husband overpowers her, but only with the consent and happy disposition of both. The sexual act in Judaism is the culmination of a loving relationship in which both partners find and share mutual satisfaction. It does not exist only for the purpose of producing children. To the contrary, the sages submitted that the beauty, character, and health of the offspring were often influenced by the nature of the sexual relations between their parents. More than that, sexual relations were not to cease after a woman's menopause. A man satisfied his conjugal obligation even if his wife was sterile or if she suffered from a disability that made conception impossible.

One of the worst obscenities was cohabitation without the spiritual components of love and consideration for one another. In Jewish mysticism, "the bond between male and female is the secret of true faith" (*Zohar*, Genesis 101b).

Jewish law provided specifically that a wife should use cosmetics and wear ornaments that would make her attractive to her husband not only in her youth but also in her old age. One of the leading authorities of medieval Jewry added, "Let a curse descend upon a woman who has a husband and does not strive to be attractive" (Meir of Rothenberg, *Responsa* 199).

On the matter of birth control, Judaism was far in the vanguard of the current moral climate. If a woman's life was at risk, or if the health of the child was in jeopardy, or if there were negative hereditary or environmental factors, the rabbis not only permitted but in some cases required methods of contraception. Never, however, did they advocate total abstention.

Procreation was most assuredly a serious responsibility in marriage, but love and companionship were at least as important in Jewish tradition. The sages reminded their students that Eve was created to be a "helper" to Adam, since in the words of God himself, "It is not good that the man should be alone . . ." (Gen. 2:18). Only later on, after they had known and loved each other, did God command them both to "be fruitful and multiply . . ." (Gen. 1:28).

In commenting on Genesis 24:67, "And Isaac brought Rebecca into his mother's tent and took Rebecca and she became his wife and he loved her," Rabbi Samson Raphael Hirsch suggested that, from the order of the verbs, we might conclude that Isaac's love for Rebecca came after his marriage to her. In modern life, we would place "he loved her" first and write "Isaac loved Rebecca and he took her and she became his wife." But however important it is that love shall precede marriage, it is far more important that it shall continue after marriage. For Judaism, sexual relations are a vital component for a lasting loving relationship.

*Christianity.*   Nearly all Christians believe that marriage between one man and one woman provides the only appropriate context for sexual intercourse. (There is some dispute about whether same-sex couples might also participate in marriage, but we shall save exploration of that question for chapter 9.) Marriage is understood as part of the created order; it is a good and natural state for human beings. Even though there is some evidence of polygamy in the Old Testament, Christians believe that God intends marriage to be between two people, who commit themselves to live in an exclusive covenant for a lifetime. Traditionally Christians have articulated three functions for marriage as an exclusive, lifetime covenant, and have used three Latin words to summarize these functions: *fides*, *proles*, and *sacramentum.*

*Fides* means faithfulness, and it refers to the role that marital stability plays in contributing to the well-being of society at large. Because marriage partners live in covenant faithfulness with one another for a lifetime, marriage provides a stable context within which marriage partners can thrive. It provides a safe, nurturing environment for rearing children and caring for other family members. Sexual fidelity is understood to provide an appropriate context for sexual activity that discourages promiscuity and prostitution. In this sense, marriage is also understood as a remedy for sin. Because marriage is one of the foundational institutions of civil society, these goods achieved within the marital covenant contribute to the stability and flourishing of the social order. In other words, a society in which individuals live in safe, stable, nurturing relationships; avoid prostitution; and are discouraged from abandoning family members who rely on them is a better society than one that lacks these goods.

*Proles* refers to the good of procreation. The union between husband and wife, when it is within the will of God, includes the good of bearing and rearing children. Marriage is a hospitable environment for receiving children and for nurturing them, as one wedding liturgy explains, "in the knowledge and love of the Lord."[4] The family is understood to provide the primary context in which children are cared for and come to know the love of God. The procreative function of marriage has led to a controversy concerning the morality of contraception. The Roman Catholic Church has articulated the view that since God intends human sexuality for procreation, anyone who uses artificial contraception intentionally separates sexual activity from its procreative end and, therefore, violates the will of God. Every instance of sexual intercourse should therefore be open to the possibility of conception, unless it is prevented by some natural means. Protestant theology has generally been more open to artificial contraception. Sometimes this openness is rooted in the belief that a marriage must be open to procreation but not in every instance of sexual activity. At other times Protestant openness to artificial contraception has grown from concerns about population growth, social justice, or a desire to prevent the transmission of genetic diseases to new generations.

*Sacramentum* refers to the bond of permanent union between husband and wife and to the abiding, sacrificial love that they share. This is the good of marriage that includes the mutual joy and delight that marriage partners take in one another, the deep communion that they share with one another, and the care and affection that they have for one another in both prosperity and adversity. Whereas *fides* and *proles* refer to social and familial goods, *sacramentum* is an interpersonal good.

Christians hold a very high view of marriage as a permanent covenant between two people, but it is not the only sexually faithful mode of life endorsed by the tradition. Christians also believe that some individuals are called to celibacy, an unmarried life free from sexual activity. The freedom from marital and familial obligations often allows celibate individuals to undertake special ministries and to cultivate more intense devotional practices. In the Roman Catholic and Eastern Orthodox traditions individuals who are gifted for a celibate life may take vows and enter a monastic community. These vows are not intended to repudiate the goodness of sexuality or of marriage but to acknowledge that human beings can live full, meaningful lives apart from sexual activity, to celebrate God's call to some individuals to live outside of marriage, and to affirm the diversity of ways of living faithfully.

The very high view of marriage held by Christians also leads to controversy regarding the permissibility of divorce and remarriage after divorce. In all cases Christians regard divorce as tragic; it is never a good, but it is sometimes permissible. The Roman Catholic Church does not permit remarriage after

4. *The Book of Common Prayer* (New York: Seabury Press, 1979), 423.

divorce but does permit a marriage to be annulled. This is essentially a decla-ration that the marriage never existed, that the relationship in which the two individuals lived—whatever it may have been—was not a Christian marriage. Protestants have accepted divorce and remarriage to varying degrees, gener-ally acknowledging that in cases of abuse or adultery a marriage covenant can be broken. Increasingly, Protestants have accepted divorce and remarriage for other reasons as well. Eastern Orthodox Christians permit divorce reluctantly for the spiritual welfare of the couple. The church must officially recognize the divorce, and then the divorced person is free to remarry. Wedding services for those remarrying include a rite of penitence and the expression of sorrow over the previous, failed marriage.

*Islam.*   In general, Muslims tend to hold traditional and conservative views regarding human sexuality. Islam teaches that sexual relations are appropri-ate only within the context of marriage. Muslim men are allowed to marry women from among the People of the Book (i.e., a Jew or a Christian), but a Muslim woman can only marry a Muslim man. This difference is due to the belief that the husband is the head of the household and the wife is expected to follow the law of his community. She must marry a fellow Muslim because it would be inappropriate for a Muslim woman to come under the authority of Judaism or Christianity. Muslim attitudes regarding the rearing of children also influence who may marry whom. Since the religion of the father typically determines the religion of the offspring, a woman should not marry a non-Muslim. There are exceptions to these norms, but this remains the general practice throughout the Islamic world.

One of the more unusual differences between the two main branches of Islam is that Shia Muslims may enter into a temporary marriage, something that is not permitted for Sunnis. This practice, called *mut'a*, allows a man and woman to become legally married for a set period of time that they mutually agree upon. After that point the marriage is dissolved, but the man is required to provide for and support any children that are conceived dur-ing the course of the marriage. This practice has been criticized by some as nothing more than a form of legalized prostitution, but its supporters argue that it is an effective way to promote individual responsibility and account-ability within society.

Because marriage between a man and a woman is the ideal state, homosex-uality is not considered to be a valid form of sexual expression in Islam. Gay and lesbian Muslims are becoming a more vocal part of the *ummah* in the modern world, particularly in the West, but they are still often marginalized by their fellow Muslims. In some countries homosexual activity is a punishable offense that is against the law, so gay Muslims in those areas must exercise discretion and caution in how they live their lives. There is no tradition of celibacy in Islam, with some texts of the Qur'an criticizing it as a lifestyle. It is therefore an expectation within Muslim societies that one will marry someone of the opposite sex and raise a family.

Birth control is generally permitted in Islam, although it is not mentioned in the Qur'an. The legitimacy of birth control is sometimes debated in the modern day, but most experts say it is permissible as long as both partners are in agreement about using it. In some countries, like Egypt, where population growth is a cause for concern, the ruling government openly promotes birth control through the media and official publications. Sterilization is generally not allowed in Islam because it alters creation from God's intended purpose and cuts off the possibility of procreation. Some who oppose birth control do so for a similar reason in that they maintain it puts humans in the place of God, who alone should have ultimate authority over the creation of human life.

Although abortion is frowned on in Islam, it is allowed when the life of the mother is in danger. In that situation it is permissible to terminate a pregnancy because the mother's life takes precedence over that of her unborn child. Legal experts disagree on when the soul enters the body and the related ethical questions regarding when human life begins. Some say it is at the moment of conception, while other argue that the fetus is not a human being until 120 days after conception. Those who hold the latter view claim that abortion is permitted up to that point but not beyond.

Local attitudes and practices regarding sexuality often play an influential role in shaping the views of Muslims who do not live in Islamic countries. For this reason, it is important to avoid overgeneralizations regarding what Muslims think about matters related to human sexuality. Despite the range of options, however, all Muslims are taught by their faith to believe that sexual expression is something healthy and good. It was given to humanity by God so that men and women might enjoy each other and perpetuate the human family.

Chapter Nine

# Current Concerns and Future Prospects

## 1. What issues are the most hotly debated by followers of the religion?

*Judaism.*   Clearly, one of the most hotly debated issues in Judaism, as in almost all religious circles, is homosexuality. Orthodox and Conservative Judaism rest their opposition to gay and lesbian rights on the biblical prohibition of *toevah* (abomination), which they conclude was a reference to homosexual behavior. Same-gender sexual activity therefore was and remains a defiance of divine will.

Reform Judaism, however, appeals to a broader understanding of the biblical term. *Toevah* in the biblical context alludes not to general homosexuality but to cultic prostitution. What is abominable for the homosexual is what is abominable for the heterosexual. Promiscuity, coercion, rape, sexual exploitation, and infidelity are all abominations. What is abominable for people of all sexual orientations is disrespect for another human being.

As Rabbi Harold Schulweis has noted, the Bible is rooted in history and history changes. In the time of the Bible, the laws of leprosy were based on the assumption that it was contagious and that it was a punishment for sins. But they did not know then of Hansen's disease; they did not know that it was not contagious. Knowing what we do today, who would treat the leper according to the faulty presupposition of knowledge in that period of time?

In addition, according to early rabbinic understanding, a deaf mute was considered to be retarded, mentally incompetent, an imbecile not qualified to serve or witness or be counted in the minyan or able to contract marriage or divorce. Again, that judgment was grounded on empirically false data. We now know that the impaired speech and hearing of deaf mutes relates in no way to their native intelligence or accountability. In many jurisdictions, therefore, we changed the laws that applied to them.

Similarly, the biblical mind knew nothing of genetically conditioned gays and lesbians who had no control over their sexual orientation. They assumed that sexual identity was a matter of personal choice and free will. The sages were scientifically in error. Their judgment then cannot be acceptable now without careful review.

Another issue that divides the Jewish community is the definition of Jewish identity with particular reference to patrilineal descent. According to traditional Jewish law, an individual can be Jewish by birth only as the child of a Jewish mother. The father's identity is irrelevant. This distinction is a rather curious one, especially in the context of biblical Judaism, wherein Jewish identity is a matter of patrilineal descent. Clearly, that culture is a patriarchal one in which ancestral lines are traced through the father's family, not the mother's. Traditionally, the people of Israel are the children of Abraham, Isaac, and Jacob, not Sarah, Rebecca, Rachel, and Leah. Even in contemporary observance, a Jew is called to the reading of the Torah, again in the most traditional circles, by his Hebrew name, which links him to his father, not his mother.

Most scholars agree that the practice of associating identity with the mother probably originated in the Middle Ages, when Jewish communities were frequently attacked and terrorized in pogroms by hordes of angry mobs. Very often those murderous assaults included the rape of Jewish women, whose subsequent children were born without knowing who the father was. In order to ensure the survival and continuity of Jewish life (and the legal legitimacy of the children), the authorities very likely decreed that Jewish identity would follow the faith of the mother, whose identity was unmistakable. Since then, in most Jewish circles, a child is considered a Jew if he/she is born of a Jewish mother.

In 1983, however, in response to the increasing incidence of mixed marriage, Reform Judaism issued a statement on patrilineal descent in which it declared that a person could be Jewish by either parent. Although it justified its pronouncement by reference to the historical past cited above, Orthodox and Conservative authorities roundly condemned this departure from the norm, insisting that it would confuse the issue of Jewish identity beyond repair. The debate continues even as these words are written.

Still another issue of continuing controversy is the rights of non-Orthodox Jews in Israel. Although separation of church and state does not exist in Israel as we know it in America, freedom of religion is a fundamental principle of political life. Every religious community enjoys complete autonomy under the officially recognized leadership of its own appointed authority. Indeed, Israel stands alone in the entire Middle East in protecting the right of every religious community to practice its faith without interference.

The Jewish religious community is governed by the Orthodox Chief Rabbinate only because the Israeli government empowers them for that purpose for political considerations. As a result, the non-Orthodox segment of the Jewish community must abide by Orthodox regulations in all matters of personal status governing marriage, divorce, and conversion. Nonetheless, non-Orthodox Jews have repeatedly challenged the exclusive monopoly of Orthodox authorities in these areas and have achieved a notable measure of success in their litigation before the Israel Supreme Court. Israel inevitably will recognize and respect the diversity of Jewish religious life within its own borders even as it already does everywhere else in the world.

*Christianity.*   There are many hotly debated issues among Christians, including the morality of abortion, environmentalism, the ordination of women, and the relationship between faith and culture. Here we shall cover just two of the most contested issues: the moral status of homosexuality and styles of worship.

The moral status of homosexuality is among the most hotly debated questions among Christians today. The Bible says very little about homosexuality and nothing at all about the moral status of lifelong, monogamous same-sex partnerships. Christians disagree about what the Bible means when it does speak of homosexuality and about what theology of human sexuality is most faithful to the biblical witness. Christians also disagree about what contributions natural and social sciences might make to our understanding of this moral question.

There are five biblical texts that mention sexual relations between two men, and one additional text that includes a reference to lesbianism. What these texts mean and how they bear on the question of same-sex covenants remains under debate. The first text, Genesis 19:5, recalls an incident in which the residents of Sodom demanded that Lot send his houseguests out into the crowd so that they might be raped. Lot refuses and sends his daughters instead. Although this account becomes the basis for the term "sodomy," most Christians acknowledge that what is condemned in Sodom is not homosexual sex but rather rape and inhospitality. The second and third texts come from the book of Leviticus (18:22 and 20:13) and state that it is an "abomination" punishable by death for a man to have sexual relations with another man as he would with a woman. The meaning of these texts is unclear for two reasons. First, they may refer to fertility rites associated with the cult of Ba'al, and the primary sin condemned is idolatry rather than homosexual acts. Second, these texts are surrounded by laws prohibiting acts that Christians no longer regard as sinful, such as wearing clothing made from blended fabric.

The remaining three texts come from the New Testament. Romans 1:26–27 argues that homosexual acts, including lesbianism, violate nature and proceed from sinful lust. The meaning of this Scripture is also debated. Did Paul refer only to those who were naturally heterosexual, but who abandoned their "nature" in favor of same-sex encounters? Or does Paul categorize all homosexual sex as a violation of nature? First Corinthians 6:9 and 1 Timothy 1:9–10 are vice lists that include the condemnation of homosexual sex along with other sins such as murder, lying, and drunkenness. What is disputed in these texts is whether the terms translated as "homosexual" referred to all same-sex acts or not. The two terms employed may have referred to male, temple prostitutes and their customers.

Disputes about the meaning of these biblical texts along with information gleaned from natural and social sciences and from experience have led Christians to a variety of conclusions about homosexuality. Here we briefly cover just three. Many Christians have concluded that the Bible clearly teaches that heterosexuality is the natural state for human beings, and that homosexuality is a tragic deviation from God's intentions. Though the biblical texts may sometimes be ambiguous, every text that refers to homosexuality condemns it. The only models for human sexual activity affirmed in the Bible are marriage and celibacy. On this view, the church should welcome and minister to homosexual persons, expecting them to live celibate lives.

A second view holds that the Bible does provide a normative, heterosexual vision for human sexuality, but that it does not condemn lifelong, same-sex covenants because it does not address this question at all. The Bible condemns idolatry, prostitution, and rape, but has nothing to say about gay marriage. On this second view, ideal human sexuality is ordered in a heterosexual way, but God graciously accommodates those who find themselves with a homosexual orientation. These individuals may fulfill the goods of marriage (see chap. 8) in lifelong same-sex relationships modeled on Christian marriage.

A third view of the moral status of homosexuality finds that it is simply a natural variation within human sexuality. Gay men and lesbians may marry one another, living in relationships that are true Christian marriages, rather than in less-than-ideal relationships that represent a divine accommodation for the tragedy of the fall.

A second issue that is hotly debated among Christians concerns worship practices. Most Christians, including Eastern Orthodox, Roman Catholic, and Protestants, worship in a manner structured according to an ancient pattern called the ordo. The ordo revolves around practices of gathering, proclamation, the sacrament of the Lord's Supper, and rituals of sending. Within this structure there are forms of prayer for confessing sin, praising and thanking

God, and bringing petitions before God. Likewise, there are traditional forms for declaring that sin has been forgiven, for exchanging signs of peace with one another, and for receiving blessings. These ancient patterns have sustained the church for centuries, and many Christians find that joining with the church throughout the ages in this form of worship helps them to become aware of God in their midst and shapes them for Christian life. But other Christian congregations have found these traditional forms to be rigid and staid; they find traditional worship does not make them aware of the presence of God in their midst and feels alienating for those new to Christianity. These congregations often employ a more contemporary form of worship that might include performances by a band with electric guitars and drum sets and congregationally sung praise songs as well as sermons and prayers. Such services would typically not include the recitation of an ancient creed, the celebration of the Lord's Supper, or other traditional elements of worship. This debate among Christians about what is the best way to worship has sometimes been described as "the worship wars."

*Islam.*    Many of the most important issues Muslims are currently trying to address can be traced back to one fundamental question: What should be Islam's relationship with the non-Muslim world? Some form of that question has been on the minds of Muslims ever since the Prophet Muhammad urged his fellow Meccans to reject polytheism and embrace worship of the one God. Muslims have tried to answer it at critical junctures in the *ummah*'s history whenever the presence of the Other was obvious and unavoidable: in the seventh century, when Islam spread into areas previously under Byzantine control; in the eighth through fifteenth centuries, when Muslims lived side-by-side with Jews and Christians in Spain; in the eleventh century when the Crusaders first arrived in Jerusalem; and in the nineteenth and twentieth centuries, when many Muslim lands were occupied by European imperial powers.

At no point in history has the question been more urgent or vital than it is today. We now live in a global environment in which it is possible to see things happening as they occur in another part of the world thousands of miles away. Advancements in technology and communication have connected us to each other in ways that people living only one hundred years ago could not have imagined in their wildest dreams. The world has grown smaller, and that is a development that holds incredible opportunity for people to come together and learn from each other.

At the same time, this is a new reality that can also exacerbate the problems and deepen the divisions that exist between people. We are now more immediately and fully aware of how "other" the Other can be. It is this situation that Islam, and every other religion, finds itself in. The differences among religions and cultures are more noticeable now than ever before and can cause some to see others as a potential threat to their way of life and belief system.

Many of their community's prior contacts with non-Muslims, especially Westerners, were marred by problems and tensions, thus causing modern-day Muslims to adopt a cautious, sometimes suspicious, approach toward relations with them. Part of this is due to the conservative nature of Islam, which sees the life of the Prophet Muhammad as the ideal example of how to live as a Muslim. This is why the hadith material, which records Muhammad's words and actions, has played such an influential role in the faith lives of individual Muslims. Anything that appears to oppose or call into question that prophetic model is viewed warily as a possible challenge to Islam and its followers. Certain facets of Western culture are perceived in just this way by some Muslims, who think too much influence from the West will undermine Islam.

It is impossible for Muslims to shut themselves off from the rest of the world, so one of their most essential tasks in modern times has been to determine how they should interact with non-Muslims. It is a complicated issue with many facets, and each community or individual addresses it in a unique way. For some, especially those who do not live in Islamic countries, the perceived secularization of Western society is a major concern. How can one be a faithful Muslim in a non-Muslim land? How should children be raised in such an environment? In some Islamic countries the Westernization of their societies through means like the Internet, media, music, and dress has been met with skepticism and apprehension. Some see these influences as a new form of colonialism that will ultimately turn Muslims, particularly young people, away from Islam and into the arms of the waiting West, which will exploit and corrupt them.

As Muslims are exposed to the ideas and practices of other cultures they are challenged to reconsider their own attitudes and ways of doing things. This inevitably leads to disagreements and debates, but it is a healthy way of addressing issues of common concern and coming to a fuller understanding of one's own identity and that of the other. Interesting and important conversations are taking place among Muslims around the world as they consider basic areas of human interaction like politics, economics, law, social customs, and the role of women in society.

In the final analysis, the question of identity is at the heart of many of the discussions currently taking place within Islam. What role does Islam play in the modern world? What does it mean to be a Muslim today? Some parts of the answers to those questions have remained unchanged for centuries and will still be pertinent centuries from now. But other parts are in need of change and refinement as Islam finds itself responding to new contexts and circumstances. Like any religion it must adapt and grow, or it runs the risk of being incapable of addressing the concerns and needs of its adherents.

## 2. What is the biggest challenge facing the religion today?

*Judaism.*   One of the major challenges facing the future vitality of Judaism in America is the increasing incidence of mixed marriage. The more reliable estimates of marital unions between Jews and non-Jews now range as high as 40 percent. Despite the efforts to stem the tide of such matches, the trend is likely to continue if not accelerate, given the mobility and openness of American society.

Although most reliable studies suggest that in the vast majority of cases in which the non-Jewish spouse converts to Judaism, the children of such marriages are raised as Jews, the outcome is not nearly so encouraging in cases where there is no conversion. Nearly three-quarters of children raised in such families go on to marry non-Jews themselves, and only 4 percent of these raise their own children as Jews. As for their links with Jewish life, only a minority of children raised by dual-religion parents identify themselves with Judaism or with the institutions of the Jewish community. Like their parents, most tend not to join synagogues, contribute to Jewish causes, visit Israel, or participate in Jewish rituals as often as do the children of in-married families.

In any event, whatever the implications of mixed marriage, its current phenomenal growth will inevitably alter the current patterns of Jewish belief and practice. Much will depend on the frequency of non-Jewish spouses converting to Judaism and thereby ensuring a better prospect for Jewish continuity in their own households. Curiously enough, a marriage in which one partner is a Jew by choice usually results in ties to Judaism equally as strong as those in a marriage in which both partners are Jews by birth.

One of the most compelling challenges in determining the future form and content of Judaism in America is the impact of Israel. For Jews in the Diaspora, Israel has served variously as a source of identity, peoplehood, pride, and dignity and as a potential haven or a spiritual center; for many others, Israel is a surrogate for Judaism, if not a "secular" religion. For Israel, Jews in America and in other Western democracies represent an irreplaceable source of economic, moral, and political support. They are also the most fertile prospects for future immigration as well as for intellectual, scientific, and technological assistance. Israel and Diaspora Jewry, especially American Jewry, are mutually interdependent. Each is essential to the other, and each exerts a reciprocal influence and cultural pull on the other.

At the same time, the two communities are not without their disagreements. Some observers attribute those differences and difficulties to problems in "communication." In most instances, however, they do not entail problems of language; rather they reflect important differences on basic issues of ideology.

Frequently, those rifts evolve out of conflicting expectations about the goals and purposes of a Jewish state. For many American Jews, the policies of a Jewish state cannot be divorced from the moral mandate of Jewish faith. For most Israelis, the requirements of nationhood and those of Judaism are entirely separate. And in the eyes of many, both in Israel and the Diaspora, "ne'er the twain shall meet."

Few will challenge the proposition that Israel will continue to play a central role in Jewish life. The real question is whether or not that role will exhaust all other indigenous creative ventures within American Jewry. Certainly the centrality of Israel is paramount in providing physical and spiritual insurance for Jews in the Diaspora, and in serving as an immediate haven for those Jewish communities already in distress.

Israel also serves as the world center to preserve, embody, and renew Jewish traditions and values; to preserve and perpetuate Jewish history; and to infuse new life into Jewish culture. It is the central address for Jewish existence in the world today that binds all Jews into a single, unified community.

This mutual responsibility among Jews in America, Israel, and elsewhere is not just a theoretical proposition for public debate. It is a major building block for more intelligent and productive insights into the meaning of Jewish identity. The horizon of the American Jew is no longer limited by two oceans. It now encompasses the whole world.

Although the depth of their convictions and the quality of their Jewish lives will depend on their own initiative as well as circumstances impossible to anticipate, American Jews will still find inspiration in knowing that their covenant with God has endured the best and worst of times. With sufficient faith and determination, it always will.

*Christianity.* The unity of the Christian church is one of the most significant challenges that Christians face today. The Nicene Creed, one of the church's oldest confessions of faith, affirms that the church is "one, holy, catholic, and apostolic." The church, in other words, is the holy institution called to unity by God in all times (apostolic) and all places (catholic). Yet the church has also always encompassed vast diversity in belief and practice.

Ideally, faithful diversity lends vitality to the church as Christians in different contexts learn from one another through respectful dialogue. A church with global scope and deep historical roots will inevitably find that its faith comes to expression in a wide variety of ways. But diversity within Christianity has often led to strife, and Christians have been as likely to cast aspersions on those who practice their faith differently as they have been to celebrate and learn from them. Deep differences in belief and practice led to the schism between East and West as well as the fracturing of the Roman Catholic Church during the Protestant Reformation, and in both cases Christians found little patience for developing resources to affirm unity in the midst of diversity.

The twentieth century, however, brought renewed interest in Christian unity. The ecumenical movement, which began to grow during the late nineteenth century, blossomed in the twentieth and found institutional expression in the World Council of Churches, founded in 1948. In its Second Vatican Council, the Roman Catholic Church expressed a deep commitment to Christian reconciliation. A number of Protestant denominations have sought to restore full communion among themselves. Most Eastern Orthodox communions participate in the World Council of Churches as it seeks ways for Christians to share ministries, worship, and evangelism.

Massive global poverty represents a second significant challenge to the Christian faith. As industrialized nations grow increasingly wealthy and developing nations struggle with poverty, illiteracy, and disease, faithfulness calls Christians to respond with compassion and even self-sacrifice. Jesus cared for and identified with outcasts in his healing and teaching ministries. Christians are called, in imitation of Christ, to seek the welfare of "the least of these." The fact that so many Christians live in wealthy, industrialized nations whose wealth historically was built on the oppression of others represents a crisis of faith and faithfulness if those Christians fail to exert strong, coordinated pressure on their governments to redress injustices globally. Christians are also called to organize ministries of the church to reach out to those in need. Preaching the gospel is only complete when it is accompanied by efforts to bring economic justice, education, and health care to those mired in poverty, illiteracy, and disease.

Emerging health-care technologies represent a third significant challenge to Christian churches. Medical advances, especially at the beginning and end of life, pose serious moral questions that Christian ethics struggles to respond to. New treatments are increasingly able to extend life and to continue life beyond what seems to be the time for a natural death. Artificial respirators and feeding tubes can maintain life even in those with virtually no brain function.

These technologies leave Christians asking, When is preserving life a good to be pursued and when does it represent a failure to trust in God? Expensive therapies such as organ transplants also raise questions about the justice of access to health care and the distribution of health-care resources. Advances in infertility treatments also raise significant challenges for Christian moral theology. As medical researchers discover new ways to assist the infertile with artificial means of conception and new ways to manipulate human DNA, questions are raised about what limits Christian faith might impose on our desire to modify our genetic makeup and to select for and against the characteristics parents wish for their children to have.

*Islam.*    The most immediate challenge facing Muslims today is terrorism. Violence done in the name of religion is not a problem unique to Islam, but no other faith in recent times has had to struggle more with the reality and effects of terrorism. It has been a divisive issue within the Muslim community, and it has had a negative impact on Islam's reputation throughout the world. For many non-Muslims, Osama bin Laden or the suicide bomber has become the quintessential face of Islam, which is often equated with intolerance, hatred, and aggression.

In fact, the overwhelming majority of Muslims disavow religious violence and believe that it goes against the spirit of their faith. They reject the message of hostility espoused by al-Qaeda and similar groups as a misguided perversion of Islam's call for peace and harmony among all people. They maintain that the Qur'an and other Muslim sources have been misinterpreted and distorted by terrorists to legitimize atrocious acts that violate the core principles of the faith. Countless Muslims of good will have come together and have joined with like-minded people from other religions to denounce those who support and justify violent acts in the name of faith. It is not uncommon to hear Muslims and others say that Islam itself has been hijacked.

Despite the efforts to condemn violence and restore the good name of Islam the fact remains that terrorist acts continue to be associated with it. The attack on the United States on September 11, 2001, is the most notorious recent example, but other incidents can be cited from around the globe. The Philippines, Bali, Indonesia, Kenya, Pakistan, Spain, and England are just a few of the other countries that have experienced first-hand the horrifying and tragic results of Islamic terrorism.

Another part of the world that is commonly added to that list is the Middle East, particularly those involved in the Israeli/Palestinian conflict. While it is true that much of the violence found there has appealed to Islam for support, it would be a mistake to equate it with the events of 9/11 or similar attacks. The problems between the Palestinians and Israelis are the result of many historical, social, cultural, and political factors that have contributed to the hostilities. Religion has played a role on both sides of the conflict, and all parties bear some responsibility for the state of affairs, so most observers argue that the situation is too complex to ascribe simply to Islamic extremism. In other words, it is important for non-Muslims to differentiate among different types of violence or terrorism done in the name of religion.

It is also essential that non-Muslims make a distinction between Islamic terrorism and terrorist acts done by Muslims. The former makes an explicit appeal to Islam to endorse or defend terrorist activities. Osama bin Laden's justification for the 9/11 attacks is a prime example of this. In his 1998 fatwa titled "Jihad against Jews and Crusaders," he lays out his case against the United States by citing the Qur'an, the hadith, and Islamic teaching to support his conclusion that Muslims have an individual duty to "kill Americans wherever they find them." In this way, the terrorist acts he calls for are legitimized (in his mind, at least) by Islam.

Quite different from these acts is terrorism done by Muslims. These acts of violence are undertaken by, or authorized by, individuals who happen to be Muslims, but no attempt is made to justify those acts by appealing to Islam. The crimes committed by Saddam Hussein while he was the president of Iraq fall under this category. His terrorist activity, some of it directed against his own people, is well documented, but he never attempted to defend it in religious terms. In fact, like many Middle Eastern political leaders, his style of governing was more secularist than religious in its orientation.

One of the most serious problems in this area currently facing Islam is the fact that many non-Muslims believe Muslims are not doing enough to speak out against Islamic terrorism. Some people, especially Westerners, have expressed a desire for a more vocal and united stand by Muslims against those who engage in terrorist activities. They interpret the lack of such a unified response as indicative of a preference by Muslims to look the other way when it comes to terrorism. Such a reaction, while understandable at times, misreads the situation and neglects the real reason that a strong Muslim voice opposed to terrorism is lacking. Unlike certain other religious groups, Islam lacks a hierarchy or centralized authority that can function as a mouthpiece to give the *ummah*'s official view on a given matter. There is no system in place that allows Muslim leaders to effectively take a position and then communicate it to the public.

This is a crucial issue that must be confronted and addressed. In fact, many Muslim leaders and organizations have spoken out against terrorism and have denounced specific acts of violence. The problem has been a lack of effective communication. One of the most significant challenges facing the Islamic community today is figuring out ways to make sure its antiterrorism message is heard by as wide an audience as possible.

## 3. What might the future have in store for the religion and its followers?

*Judaism.*   Whatever the future holds for American Judaism, no analysis or prognosis can ignore two decisive factors. One of them is the rapidly aging population of the American Jewish community. American Jews face an alarmingly low birth rate. Whether the explanation may be attributed to greater sexual freedom, fewer and later marriages, more divorces, or lower fertility, the trend implies a sharply declining Jewish population in the future. Continuing low fertility rates mean that the number of children in the communal pipeline will soon drop sharply, causing a corresponding decline in enrollments in Jewish schools and other institutions for young people.

Quantity may not be as crucial as quality, but certain basic components of community well-being, such as education; social services for youth, families, and the elderly; defense agencies; and support for Israel and cultural vitality all depend on a certain critical mass in numbers. It may not require six million Jews to ensure a spiritual vitality in America, but it will not be sustained by half that number or less. Essential operations of religious and cultural institutions require certain minimal levels of funding and active participation, and those levels in turn depend on a crucial base of constituents. The closing of synagogues in smaller communities across the country for lack of adequate membership demonstrates the malady brought on by demographic change and shrinking numbers.

In contrast to falling birth rates and an aging population, the future of Jewish life in America is also likely to reflect a significant increase in the number of non-Jews converting to Judaism. If Judaism has forever been shaped and guided by the cultural conditioning of Jews who maintained it, the contours of Judaism will inevitably change to reflect the experience of many people who became Jews by choice and not by birth. Perceptions about Jewish history, Jewish holidays, and Jewish life-cycle ceremonies will obviously be different for those individuals without any Jewish ancestors than for those with such roots. Educational assumptions and curricula cannot be the same for children with one set of grandparents who are Jewish and another set who are not. The notion of Jewish "peoplehood" will obviously evoke different associations for Jews by birth and Jews by choice.

The likely outcome then for Jews in America is that in the future Judaism will reflect much more a spiritual character than an ethnic one. Even though the cultural component remains a powerful ingredient in Jewish identity, Judaism is becoming for most Jews far more a religious association. Even for Jews by birth, ethnicity is much less significant than it was for the earlier immigrant generations.

Although the ties that bind Jews to Israel cut across all generational lines, they are far less binding among younger Jews. Barely 20 percent of all American Jews have ever visited Israel, and the vast majority of those are older people. Though contributions to Jewish cultural causes still approach earlier levels of giving, older generations are far more generous than younger ones. Unlike their parents and grandparents, the new generation of American Jews does not share the memories and experiences of recent climactic turning points in Jewish history. For most of them, the Holocaust is an event of the distant past, like the Civil War might be for all older Americans. It is even difficult for almost all of them to remember a world in which there never was a Jewish state.

In most cases, Judaism is for younger Jews a matter of celebrating holidays and festivals, including a menorah on Chanukah, a seder on Passover, and maybe fasting on Yom Kippur and an occasional Sabbath experience. It includes the observance of life-cycle events from B'rit Milah (circumcision) and baby naming to bar/bat mitzvah to marriage and death. These are essentially religious acts, if not directly inspired by spiritual ideals, then at least respectful of them. This new generation of American Jews may not all choose the synagogue as the venue for their Jewish activity and instead may opt for smaller fellowships and/or study groups, but they will think of themselves largely as another faith community on the American landscape.

The attempt to define the meaning and significance of Judaism for any given generation is an extremely risky venture. Even if it reflects the prevailing trends of the time, it will always be subject to change. How future events and circumstances will alter the analysis and prognosis just completed belongs entirely in the realm of speculation. It would be foolish to pretend that previous patterns of change are entirely useless in forecasting future ones, but it would also be futile to chart precisely the course that Jewish life is likely to follow.

We may only pray that the best is yet to be.

*Christianity.*   Christian theology teaches that the kingdom of God has begun and is in our midst even now, but also that it has not yet fully come. Christians, in other words, believe that they live between the "already" and the "not yet." Christians live in the meantime and look forward to a future that brings God's final triumph over evil. What Christians believe the future holds in store sets the agenda for how they are to act here and now. Christians believe that in the kingdom of God, the earth is renewed and restored to its pristine state, human beings are resurrected and live—body and soul—in peace and love, and all aspects of creation, including the plants and animals, live in harmony and beauty. Since Christians are to live now in joyful anticipation of God's coming reign, they are to work for reconciliation and justice, bodily and spiritual health, and ecologically responsible policies that reflect that future. Because the Christian faith also teaches that in the kingdom of God all people will affirm and joyfully submit to the lordship of Jesus Christ, Christians work to proclaim the good news of the gospel to all people.

Aside from these theological descriptions of what Christians believe the future holds, we can identify some descriptive possibilities. For instance, the Christian faith will most likely continue to grow in areas geographically and culturally different from Europe and North America. Both conflict and renewal will likely grow as Christians from Asia, Africa, Oceania, and Latin America become more prominent and Christians in Europe and North America become increasingly aware of the global context of the Christian faith. As Christians seek a unified faith in the midst of diverse cultural forms, they will need to engage in sustained conversations and interactions with one another. These sustained engagements will likely have an impact on both belief and practice. Christian theologians will need to find ways to accommodate diverse expressions of Christian belief, especially as that diversity emerges from historical and cultural differences. Likewise, worship and ministry practices may evolve as different global contexts begin to influence one another. These developments in belief and practice will inevitably bring some conflict, but they also contain the seeds of significant renewal for the church.

Developments in global Christianity may well fuel a continued quest for unity, such as is found in the ecumenical movement. Attention to differences in culture and language as well as diversity in belief and practice may prompt Christians to seek what unites them and to affirm with renewed vigor the catholicity of the church. Already ecumenical conversations between Roman Catholics and Eastern Orthodox churches have proven productive. Lutheran churches and the Roman Catholic Church have also worked to develop theological documents that affirm their mutual faithfulness while also respecting continuing differences. Other Protestant denominations are seeking to establish or restore full communion among themselves.

Often this ecumenical spirit has been coupled with interest in liturgical renewal and reform. Christians often find that they are able to agree on ways to worship together even when they differ on the finer points of doctrine. In the future we may see the development of an increasing number of inter-denominationally shared liturgies. The basic structure of the ordo may provide a framework that brings unity to the diverse ways in which different Christian traditions develop the prayers, sermons, sacraments, and acts of reconciliation included in worship.

Finally, the future may bring renewed interest in Christian critique and reform of culture. Throughout much of the twentieth century, Christians, especially in Europe and North America, held a dominant and privileged place in society. But the latter parts of that century and the early twenty-first century have brought increasing attention to deep social pluralism. Christians, moreover, have had to acknowledge that their dominant place, especially in American society, very often did not mean that the Christian values of justice, concern for the poor and outcast, and respect for all persons became the dominant values of their society. The fusion of faith and culture did more to blunt the prophetic edge of the Christian faith than it did to critique and transform the culture. As American Christians in particular become increasingly aware of the pluralism of their society, some may seek to reassert their dominance and to reunite faith and nationalism. But others may take the opportunity to recover the prophetic voice of the faith so that they are able with increased integrity to call into question abuses of power and privilege, to seek justice and reconciliation, and to propose reforms that cohere with Christian commitments to uphold the poor, the outcast, the weak, and the powerless.

*Islam.*   Islam is the fastest-growing religion in the world, and well over one billion people now profess it as their faith. There are no indications that its rate of growth is slowing down, so it is safe to assume that it will continue to play a major role on the world stage. If the total number of followers a religion has can serve as a benchmark for what is to come, the future of Islam looks bright and healthy. In addition to those who are born into the *ummah*, countless individuals convert to Islam every day, demonstrating its appeal and attraction as a way of life.

While the content and expression of Islamic faith are unlikely to change, Muslims may find they will need to adapt in certain areas if things continue to go in the direction they appear to be headed. One area concerns Muslim presence in non-Muslim countries, especially Western nations. Recent years have seen a remarkable increase in the number of Muslims in Western Europe. In many countries, Islam is now the second largest religion, and the total number of Muslims is approaching the number of practicing Christians. While the Muslim populations of the United States and Canada do not reach those same percentages, they are still a significant minority within those countries.

One of the challenges for Muslims living in these places concerns how to live side-by-side with others who do not share one's faith or view of appropriate social discourse regarding matters of religion. Freedom of expression and free speech are among the most cherished liberties of Western societies, and the right to say what is on one's mind extends into the area of religion. This is an unfamiliar concept to many Muslims who are new arrivals in these countries. When they hear people speak critically of religion, or Islam in particular, they sometimes take it personally and feel offended.

At times, Muslims who have spent their entire lives in non-Muslim countries can have a similar reaction to perceived offenses against Islam. A much publicized recent example was the murder in Holland of the filmmaker Theo van Gogh, a distant relative of the famous painter. He was killed by a Dutch-born Muslim with Moroccan citizenship who thought one of van Gogh's films disrespects Islam. Another example of the same phenomenon can be seen in the anger and violence that erupted among Muslims in response to political cartoons published in a Danish newspaper and reprinted in other European periodicals, for they felt these demeaned and insulted the Prophet Muhammad.

More and more Muslims will find themselves living among non-Muslims in countries that permit the expression of personal views that can be deemed insulting by others, and the potential for violence will remain very real. While it is the responsibility of all parties to conduct themselves in ways that respect the rights and feelings of others, Muslims must continue to develop effective means of communicating their concerns that are within the bounds of society's norms and laws.

Another recent development likely to have an impact on the future shape and direction of the religion is the growing influence of political groups that are affiliated with Islam. Such organizations have been around for a long time, but they have become more actively involved in the official political process of late. As already noted, the strong showing by the Muslim Brotherhood in Egypt's most recent parliamentary election was an outcome that surprised many. More shocking was the overwhelming victory of Hamas in the Palestinian elections that catapulted into power a group known more for terrorism than for sitting around the negotiation table. It is too soon to tell if the rise of such groups is a sign of things to come or a blip on the screen, but it will undoubtedly be a factor in how Muslims understand the relationship between their faith and politics.

Some observers, both Muslim and non-Muslim, believe that Islam is in need of a reformation similar to the one Christianity experienced in the sixteenth century. They maintain that Islam must turn from its focus on the past and look to the future in order to address the concerns of Muslims living in the modern world. Only in this way, goes the argument, can distorted views of the faith that endorse violence and terrorism be overcome, and the message of tolerance and respect that is at the heart of Islam be allowed to flourish.

It would be a pity, however, to limit the call for reform to Islam alone. All religions, perhaps the monotheistic ones most of all, are in need of constant renewal and transformation. Only then can their followers come together and work toward building a better world. Only then can we acknowledge and celebrate what our neighbors believe.

# Appendixes

## Important Dates for Judaism

| | |
|---|---|
| Circa 1200 BCE | Exodus of Israel from Egypt |
| 70 CE | Destruction of Jerusalem by the Roman Empire and the end of the Second Jewish Commonwealth |
| 950–1150 | Golden Age in Spain and the apex of Jewish and Islamic culture |
| 1135–1204 | Maimonides—foremost medieval, Sephardic, Jewish philosopher and commentator |
| 1492 | Expulsion of the Jews from Spain following the end of the Golden Age |
| 1567 | Publication of the Shulchan Aruch, the summary compilation of Jewish law and observance by Joseph Karo |
| 1654 | Arrival of the first twenty-three Jews to New Amsterdam and the beginning of Jewish settlement in North America |
| 1700–1760 | Israel Baal Shem Tov, founder of Hasidism |
| 1897 | First Zionist Congress convened by Theodor Herzl in Basel, Switzerland |
| 1917 | Balfour Declaration issued by Great Britain in support of a Jewish National Home in Palestine |
| 1933–45 | The systematic destruction of six million Jews by Nazi Germany during the Holocaust (Shoah) |
| 1948 | Creation of the state of Israel and restoration of Jewish sovereignty |

# Key Terms for Judaism

**halakah.**   Hebrew term for Jewish law meaning literally "the way" with reference to the "way" in which a Jew should observe Jewish teaching.

*kipah.*   A head-covering customarily used for worship and, among more observant Jews, during all other waking hours as well. Also referred to by its Yiddish term, *yamulkah.*

**kosher.**   Ritually fit or proper, which refers not only to certain prescribed foods but to ritual objects of any kind.

**minyan.**   A quorum of ten people, in Orthodoxy consisting only of men, as the minimum number required for public worship. In non-Orthodox communities, women are usually counted in the minyan.

**mitzvah.**   The Hebrew word for a deliberate act that enables a person to approximate divine activity by performing an act of ethical or spiritual distinction. It is the Jewish way to holiness.

**shabbat.**   The seventh day designated for spiritual rest and renewal, and the only holy day prescribed in the Ten Commandments.

**shalom.**   The Hebrew greeting for "hello" and "good-bye," but which also connotes more literally a sense of "wholeness," fullness," or "completeness."

**Talmud.**   The vast compendium of rabbinic law and lore, consisting of the first codification of Jewish law, the Mishnah, and its commentary, the Gemora. In most places the Babylonian Talmud, completed in the sixth century, was the basis for all further Jewish learning and teaching.

*tikun olam.*   A phrase that originated in Kabbalah (Jewish mysticism) that means "healing" or "repairing a broken world," usually associated in a modern context with acts of social justice, improving the quality of human life, or restoring existence to its original wholeness.

**Torah.**   The first of three major sections of the Hebrew Bible, which consists of Genesis through Deuteronomy. The remaining sections of *Nevi'im* (Prophets) and *Kethuvim* (Writings) complete the entire sacred document called the TaNaK.

*tzedakah.*   The Hebrew term most frequently associated with "charity" but best defined as "justice" or "righteousness." Charitable giving in Judaism is an obligation required by law as something that is right, not just kind or thoughtful.

# Internet Sites for Judaism

www.Judaism101.com
www.zipple.com
www.mesora.org
www.jewishnet.net
www.shamash.org

# Further Reading for Judaism

Dimont, Max. *Jews, God and History*. New York: Simon and Schuster, 1962.
Greenstein, Howard R. *Judaism: An Eternal Covenant*. Philadelphia: Fortress Press, 1983. Republished by Wipf and Stock Publishers, Eugene, OR.
Kertzer, Morris N. *What Is a Jew?* Revised by Lawrence A. Hoffman. New York: Maxwell Macmillan International, 1993.
Kushner, Harold S. *To Life! A Celebration of Jewish Being and Thinking*. Boston: Little, Brown, 1993.
Trepp, Leo. *A History of the Jewish Experience:* Book 1, *Torah and History;* Book 2, *Torah, Mitzvot, and Jewish Thought*. Revised and updated edition. Springfield, NJ: Behrman House, 2001.

## Important Dates for Christianity

| | |
|---|---|
| 70 CE | Destruction of Temple in Jerusalem |
| 312 | Conversion of Constantine |
| 325 | Council of Nicea |
| 726 | Iconoclast Controversy begins in Eastern Church |
| 1054 | The Great Schism |
| 1517 | Beginning of the Protestant Reformation |
| 1618–48 | 30 Years' War/Wars of Religion in Europe |
| 1948 | Founding of the World Council of Churches |
| 1962 | Beginning of the Second Vatican Council |

## Key Terms for Christianity

**Eastern Orthodox.** The beliefs and practices of churches that developed in the Eastern Roman Empire, such as the Greek Orthodox Church, or that worship using the Byzantine Rite, such as the Russian Orthodox Church. Eastern Orthodox Christians acknowledge the primacy of the patriarch of Constantinople.

**incarnation.** The Christian doctrine that affirms that Jesus Christ is fully human and fully divine. Christians believe that, in Christ, God is joined to humanity so that humankind might be redeemed.

**polity.** The way that Christian churches govern themselves. The three primary forms of polity are episcopal, congregational, and presbyterian.

**Protestant.** The beliefs and practices of the churches that split from the Roman Catholic Church during a period of reform in sixteenth-century Europe. Protestant Christians affirm the Bible as the final source of authority (*sola scriptura*), that salvation is granted solely by God's grace through the gift of faith, and the priesthood of all believers.

**Roman Catholic.** The beliefs and practices of the church as it developed in the Western Roman Empire. Roman Catholic Christians acknowledge the primacy of the bishop of Rome, the pope.

**sacrament.** A rite that serves as an outward and visible sign of an inward and spiritual grace. The Roman Catholic and Eastern Orthodox churches celebrate seven sacraments, including baptism, the Lord's Supper, marriage, ordination, confirmation (or chrismation in the Orthodox communions), anointing, and confession. Protestants celebrate baptism and the Lord's Supper.

**sin.**    Refers both to the condition of being alienated from God (original sin) and specific acts that violate the will of God.

**Trinity.**    The Christian doctrine that affirms that there is one God who consists of three persons: the Father, Son, and Holy Spirit.

## Internet Sites for Christianity

The official Web site of the Vatican: www.vatican.va/
The Greek Orthodox Archdiocese of America: www.goarch.org
The National Council of Churches. This site includes links to the Web sites of member denominations: http://nccusa.org
The World Council of Churches: www.wcc-coe.org
Ken Collins Web site, a resource for understanding Christian, especially Protestant, worship: www.kencollins.com
The Revised Common Lectionary: http://divinity.library.vanderbilt.edu/ lectionary/
World Christian Database: www.worldchristiandatabase.org

## Further Reading for Christianity

Hellwig, Monika. *Understanding Catholicism*. Mahwah, NJ: Paulist Press, 2002.
Küng, Hans. *Christianity: Essence, History, and Future*. Translated by John Bowden. New York: Continuum, 1998.
McGrath, Alister E. *An Introduction to Christianity*. Oxford: Blackwell, 1997.
Placher, William. *A History of Christian Theology: An Introduction*. Louisville, KY: Westminster/John Knox Press, 1983.
Ware, Timothy. *The Orthodox Church*. London: Penguin Books, 1997.
Weaver, Mary Jo. *Introduction to Christianity*. Belmont, CA: Wadsworth Publishing Co., 1984

# Important Dates for Islam

| | |
|---|---|
| 570 CE | Birth of Muhammad |
| 610 | Qur'an Revelations begin |
| 622 | Migration to Medina |
| 632 | Death of Muhammad |
| 661–750 | Umayyad Period |
| 750–1258 | Abbasid Period |
| 1258 | Invasion of Baghdad by the Mongols |

# Key Terms for Islam

**fatwa.**   A legal ruling, usually delivered by a mufti.

**hadith.**   The traditions that record what Muhammad said and did.

*hijra.*   The migration from Mecca to Medina made by Muhammad and a small group of followers in 622.

**imam.**   For Sunnis, this is the title given to a prayer leader. For Shia, the term designates the one who has supreme authority over their community.

*masjid.*   Literally, "place of prostration," the most common term for a mosque.

*mihrab.*   The niche in a mosque that indicates the direction of prayer toward Mecca.

*minbar.*   The pulpit in a mosque, usually located to the right of the mihrab.

*shirk.*   The worst sin in Islam, it refers to the act of associating with God something that is created.

*ummah.*   The worldwide Muslim community.

# Internet Sites for Islam

Prince Alwaleed bin Talal Center for Muslim-Christian Understanding (Georgetown University): http://cmcu.georgetown.edu/
University of Georgia megasite on Islam: http://www.uga.edu/islam/
Islamic Statements against Terrorism: http://www.unc.edu/~kurzman/terror.htm

# Further Reading for Islam

Armstrong, Karen. *Islam: A Short History*. New York: Modern Library, 2002.

Cook, Michael. *The Koran: A Very Short Introduction*. New York: Oxford University Press, 2000.

Drummond, Richard Henry. *Islam for the Western Mind: Understanding Muhammad and the Koran*. Charlottesville, VA: Hampton Roads Publishing Co., 2005.

Esposito, John L. *Islam: The Straight Path*. Revised 3rd edition. New York: Oxford University Press, 2005.

Kaltner, John. *Islam: What Non-Muslims Should Know*. Minneapolis: Fortress Press, 2003.

Tayob, Abdulkader. *Islam: A Short Introduction*. Boston: Oneworld Publications, 1999.

# About the Authors

**Howard R. Greenstein** served as rabbi of the Jewish congregation of Marco Island, Florida. Prior to that he served congregations in Florida, Ohio, and Massachusetts. Greenstein had been an adjunct professor at the University of Florida, University of North Florida, Jacksonville University, and Florida Gulf Coast University. Other books by Howard Greenstein are *Judaism: An Eternal Covenant* (1983) and *Turning Point: Zionism and Reform Judaism* (1981).

**Kendra G. Hotz** serves as adjunct professor of theology at Memphis Theological Seminary. Hotz is an ordained minister in the Presbyterian Church (U.S.A.), coauthor (with Matthew T. Mathews) of *Shaping the Christian Life: Worship and the Religious Affections* (2006), and coauthor of *Transforming Care: A Christian Vision of Nursing Practice* (2005).

**John Kaltner** is an Associate Professor of Religious Studies at Rhodes College in Memphis, Tennessee, where he teaches courses in Bible, Islam, and Arabic. Among his books are *Islam: What Non-Muslims Should Know* (Minneapolis: Fortress Press, 2003); *Inquiring of Joseph: Getting to Know a Biblical Character through the Qu'ran* (Collegeville, MN: Liturgical Press/Michael Glazier, 2003); *Ishmael Instructs Isaac: An Introduction to the Qur'an for Bible Readers* (Collegeville, MN: Liturgical Press/Michael Glazier, 1999).

CPSIA information can be obtained at www.ICGtesting.com
Printed in the USA
BVOW071824260613

324404BV00001B/10/P

9 780664 230654